When Jesus Calls

Transforming businesses into expressions of God's Kingdom

Peter Lawry

Your Kingdom come...on earth, [just] as it is in heaven.
(Matt. 6:10, NASB)

COPYRIGHT AND LEGAL PERMISSIONS

Copyright © 2021 Peter Lawry

All rights reserved. No part of this publication may be reproduced, stored in a retrieval system, or transmitted in any form or by any means – electronic, mechanical, photocopy, recording, scanning, or other – except for brief quotations in critical reviews or articles, without the prior written permission of the author.

Published by **Business As Mission Limited, New Zealand**
Company No.: 6246009
NZBN: 9429045982170
Website: https://business-as-mission.com

ISBN (Printed Book): 978-0-473-60831-6
ISBN (Kindle version): 978-0-473-60832-3
ISBN (Audiobook): 978-0-473-61483-6

Scripture quotations marked (NKJV) are taken from the Holy Bible the New King James Version® (NKJV)®. Copyright © 1982 by Thomas Nelson. Used by permission. All rights reserved.

Scripture quotations marked (NIV) are taken from the Holy Bible, New International Version®, NIV®. Copyright © 1973, 1978, 1984, 2011 by Biblica, Inc.™ Used by permission of Zondervan. All rights reserved worldwide (www.zondervan.com). "NIV" and "New International Version" are trademarks registered in the United States Patent and Trademark Office by Biblica, Inc.™

Scripture quotations marked (NASB) are taken from the (NASB®) New American Standard Bible®, Copyright © 1960, 1971, 1977, 1995, 2020 by The Lockman Foundation. Used by permission. All rights reserved. (www.lockman.org)

All contributors to this book are real persons and have confirmed in writing that the stories included are accurate. Where first and last names, company names and website addresses of contributors are included in full, these details are asserted as factually correct. Certain contributors have requested pseudonyms be used to protect either their own or third parties' privacy; in which case only a first name and country has been included (neither of which may be their own). Neither the author nor publisher, nor any other party associated with the writing and/or production of this book, accept any responsibility for errors, whether by omission or commission, in relation to contributors and/or their stories.

Editing by Debbie Watson, *Get It Right Proofreading Services*, Australia. Professional member of IPed Australia and Queensland Editors. (www.getitrightproofreading.com.au).

Author's photo by Steve Lloyd Photography. Copyright © 2019 Steve Lloyd, Rangiora, New Zealand. Used by permission. All rights reserved. (www.stevelloydphotography.com).

Cover design and artwork (image name: "His Kingdom Come") by Jene Lubbe, T/A CreativeJene, creative artist. Copyright © 2021 Jene Lubbe, Rangiora, New Zealand. Used by permission. All rights reserved. (CreativeJene@outlook.com).

Formatting by István Szabó, *Sapphire Guardian Publishing*, Budapest, Hungary. (istvan@sapphireguardian.com).

THIS BOOK IS DEDICATED TO
a first century Jewish businessman named Zac
(see Luke 19:1-10).

Enticed by a secular world, Zacchaeus abandoned early on the benefits of God's Kingdom in business. His reasons are never shared with us. Possibly it was ignorance; more likely it was deliberate choice. Either way, he made enemies of every business client, remaining at odds with them until a personal encounter with Jesus changed everything. The two spent quality time together over a meal – and a remarkable turnaround took place. Zac altered so completely that he offered not only to restore every sum of money he'd ever stolen from anyone, but to do so four times over!

I'm immensely grateful to Zac. Facing his failings, and the repentance that followed, offers me profound hope. Restorative transformation – both of ourselves and of the businesses we operate – is not only possible but imperative, and exhilarating, through Jesus.

TABLE OF CONTENTS

Reader Endorsements i
Foreword v
Preface ix
Introduction xiii
Chapter 1: "What If You Make God Your CEO?" 1
Chapter 2: Faith Isn't Optional! 5
Chapter 3: The Call (Exciting – But Beware Too!) 11
Chapter 4: The Centrality of the Kingdom 25
Chapter 5: The God-Established Business 37
Chapter 6: The Identity-Reflecting Business 45
Chapter 7: The Outrageous Business 53
Chapter 8: The Attractive Business 63
Chapter 9: The Upside-Down Business 73
Chapter 10: The Forgiving Business 83
Chapter 11: The Sacrificial Business 93
Chapter 12: The Holy Business 107
Chapter 13: The Abundant Business 123
Chapter 14: The Transforming Business 135
Chapter 15: The Resourcing Business 147
Chapter 16: The Unlimited Business 159
Chapter 17: The Miraculous Business 169
Chapter 18: The Embracing Business 177
Chapter 19: So He Alone Receives The Glory 189
Chapter 20: The Next Move Is Yours 193
Enjoy this Book? You can make a big difference. 197
Further Reading 199
Acknowledgements 201
About the Author 205

READER ENDORSEMENTS

Alistair Whitmoor-Pryer, International Trainer & Business Developer, UK (www.ashercare.co.uk)
This is a must-read book. Peter has captured the heart of God for those in business. Each page contains incredible insights, backed up by Scriptures, which will not only challenge but encourage you to make changes to the way your business operates. As you read, revelation follows revelation, helping you establish your business – or any company – with God as the CEO.

I found this book inspiring, impacting and certainly challenging in the way it presents so many amazing truths about operating business under Kingdom authority and abundance. I particularly love its fresh approach, and short, easy-to-read chapters.

God bless you richly, Peter, for your obedience in writing a book that is greatly needed in today's marketplace. A truly inspirational read.

Susan Cooney, SME Business Improvement Specialist, New Zealand (www.oxygen8.co.nz)
As I was reading *When Jesus Calls*, I visualised God being present at board meetings, team meetings, one-on-one meetings, and client meetings, because He was asked to be. I am excited! Thank you Peter, for boldly sharing your love for Him in a clear, concise way, enabling each of us to grow in our relationship with Him, stepping forward in faith to better ourselves and our businesses, thus impacting the world.

Deb Riach, Entrepreneur, MD, Coffee Worx Ltd, New Zealand (www.coffeeworx.co.nz)
I've known Peter for the past 12 years and it's been rewarding watching him find his purpose in God. Like most of us, the path isn't always straight and at times the destination seems obscured, but Peter kept seeking the right path for his gifts, skills and natural abilities; and I think this book demonstrates where God has led him.

As a long-term business owner myself, I know there are times when all of us in business feel stuck, overwhelmed or we lose focus. *When Jesus Calls* is an excellent re-focusing tool, reminding each of us, whose calling is in the business world, that we are not alone; that God is just as interested and active in our business decisions as He is in our spiritual growth.

Well written my friend. I found some real nuggets within these pages.

Stephan Rattray, Entrepreneur, MD, BG Contracting Ltd, New Zealand (www.bgcontracting.co.nz)
I've known Peter for the best part of eight years, both as fellow church members and in business. The reason I say 'best part' is that Peter has an authentic knack of bringing out the 'best' in you.

When Jesus Calls is an answer to why I am doing this. As a business owner in the age of COVID lockdowns and external control, it's easy to feel like a paper bag in the wind. Grounded in a Biblical understanding of God's call to Christians in business, and inspired with the stories of other business owners' journeys, this book is a valuable ongoing reference source – more than a one-time read.

Since reading this I have turned our business organigramme upside down to reflect the servant leadership model. This has dramatically changed the thinking and culture of our leadership team: they realise they are there to support and serve their direct reports, not exercise power over them.

Andrew Burger, retired international barrister & solicitor, South Africa, Australia & New Zealand
I've just finished this book – it was simply brilliant, and what a tribute to our Lord. I can't think when I last read a book from cover to cover with the enthusiasm I had for this gem. Every personal experience shared was an individual masterpiece, adding real-life, real-time examples to the Biblical principles revealed.

How differently I might have approached my career if I'd had this book during my practice tenure. The wisdom Peter imparts reveals God's expectations, already divinely revealed in Scripture, and now succinctly collated in this compendium. To our divine CEO be all the glory.

Jonathan Melville, Pastor, Rangiora Baptist Church, New Zealand (www.rbc.net.nz)
Peter and I come together from very different backgrounds, yet we've found ourselves drinking from the same well – the living waters of Jesus Christ. I don't claim to understand the business world: that's not been my calling. However, I do understand dry ground coming to life, as water is poured into it.

For too long, many of our endeavours, as Christians, have existed as if separate from that well. The world of business and commerce is no exception. I've pastored many business owners, and seen them become isolated in deserts of pressure, stress, compromise, or greed. Perhaps you too have recognised this? Perhaps there is a thirst in you for something life-giving?

In the pages that follow you will find an echo of Christ's invitation. Peter's book is something like a map, a guidebook of the terrain to traverse, to aid you on your own journey to drink at His well.

FOREWORD

My history and experience in the business world, as CEO, board member and owner of many multi-national businesses, should have equipped me to do well and succeed in all endeavours I put my hand to. In many cases it did, for which only God deserves the praise. But I also walked the road of failure with many initiatives and new ideas. We've all been there.

As business men and women, we cannot help but look at people who are really successful and wonder how they manage to do things better – and what we can learn from them. I'm sure you, too, have tried to find that 'cutting edge', to increase revenue, improve productivity, reduce costs, and motivate staff. The commercial world will tell you that, if you stay on a cycle of continuous improvement, rejuvenation, and self-development, your business will grow, staff will be happy, customer loyalty will continue, and new customers will flock to your business. Yet if that were so, why do we all have those lonely nights as business owners, where we lie awake constantly worrying about our bottom line, deals that are on the edge, staff welfare, and much more?

I realised only later in my business life that a big reason was that "I" was always in the centre of everything. When you build and run a successful, multi-million dollar, international business, you tend to lay a dangerous platform of personal pride. The world begins to applaud your achievements. It puts you on a pedestal; and that's a perilous place to be – there's only one way off!

I began to consider King Solomon. The Bible tells us he was the wisest man who'd ever lived; but he still failed. Yes, his leadership portrayed examples of great wisdom and success; but he also made some very serious blunders that ultimately led to the breakup of his empire. If *he* couldn't stay the course, and ultimately failed as a leader, we too will struggle to become successful leaders unless God is at our helm.

Likewise, when I examined the history of failed CEOs, I wanted to understand which mistakes had caused them to fail as corporate leaders. (Sometimes one can learn more from studying mistakes than from studying successes.) Two of their common mistakes are the myopic pursuit of wealth, and the absence of a Godly character in the way they conduct business.

As you read this amazing book, *"When Jesus Calls"*, the missing ingredient becomes so clear: *God has to become the CEO of your business!* Peter describes how he was challenged, by a wise mentor, to "make God your CEO and you become nothing more than His employee." His book unpacks the impact and results that have happened, as he – and other business owners, whose stories are included too – have done just that.

Peter, I'm so grateful for the understanding God has given you. Thank you for writing this amazing book. If I'd had it available to me during the days I was leading an organisation, I would have done things so differently.

Now to you, Peter's readers, I urge you to grasp the importance of his insights, with real intent. Change the way you lead and run your business – for God's sake, as well as your own! As Albert Einstein once said: "Do not try to become a person of success, but rather a person of value." May God bring that value in your life and business.

Many Blessings.

Jan De Lange
Serial entrepreneur, fellow businessman,
leader, and lover of Jesus.
(South Africa originally!)

PREFACE

This book is less of a 'how to' manual, and more of a 'purpose for' undertaking business God's way.

As a business improvement coach, 'the how to' of business is something I've taught for years. Yet I've come to realise that "how to" is secondary. There's a reason God calls us into business, and recognising His reason is our primary task. What value is there in setting ourselves on a path to some*thing* when we don't first understand the some*where* to which we're moving and the Some*One* who's invited us? What a folly to succeed at the wrong things! As Jesus puts it: *"What good will it be for someone to gain the whole world, yet forfeit their soul?"* (Matt. 16:26, NIV).

With this in mind, I assert business is not a commercial endeavour first and foremost – it's a heaven-motivated one. A God-inspired way of leading groups of people to interact with one another, generating resources which He (not us) uses to establish His Kingdom on earth.

The Lord's Prayer

Jesus' *Pattern for Prayer* is a goldmine for entrepreneurs and businesspeople.

I don't mean to suggest that it, nor the Bible as a whole, should be read as a commercial guidebook. Such an idea is repugnant. It limits and corrupts Scripture to something that encourages us to read into it whatever we want to read out of it. I'm saying that God is interested in every part of our lives; therefore, there is no secular/spiritual divide. Which means that everything in Scripture that's valuable for our personal, spiritual lives is equally vital for our business lives too.

Consider the Lord's Prayer. In it, Jesus taught us vital treasures; for He sees Kingdom resources (*our daily bread*) flowing from –

- our relationship with God (*Our Father in heaven*); accompanied by
- unfettered praise for God, (*Hallowed be Your Name*); as we
- recognise that God releases His resources through His Kingdom (*Your Kingdom come, Your will be done, on earth as it is in heaven*), so we may be reconciled to Him (see John 3:16).

Amazingly, we are invited to benefit from these resources too – but not as a right or a reward for effort; purely by His grace.

Traditional business is about the financial bottom line. I want to help you hear the call to much more than that. This book is therefore intended

- to lead you to a holy unrest,
- motivate you to understand the Far Bigger Reason that He's put you into leadership of a business, and
- give you the One Major Invitation that will permit you to fulfil the call He's invited you to, as a business owner. That invitation is the development of a deeper, more intimate relationship with the King of the Kingdom.

Others have kindly contributed their experiences to my own. Therefore, as you read, you'll meet several entrepreneurs and hear about their encounters with God, in their businesses. Some details of some of those stories have been changed, so inadvertent identification of third parties can be avoided, and to fulfil the requests of some contributors themselves, who prefer anonymity.

INTRODUCTION

God tolerated my first attempt at business, when I was 34. How He must have laughed, albeit graciously. Financially and momentum-wise, it never got off the ground.

My second got some lift-off, but then burned and crashed after I engaged my first staff members. I had no idea, back then, how to employ staff well, or lead them.

My third attempt did better for a while. Working with a business partner, we helped more than 50 families not eligible for bank mortgages, to move into homes funded by investors. Investors received a ROI (Return on Capital) of around 34%; and helped the homeowners to purchase an asset. It was a win-win. Our programme worked very well for two years until the property market changed, at which point I felt the need to move on. I sold my shares to my business partner for the equivalent of US$7,000 – not a capital gain to shout about, but at least on the right side of zero.

My fourth business produced my biggest crash-and-burn. After investing into multiple franchise territories, I employed completely the wrong operations manager. My company failed because I failed. I was well-intentioned but was playing a game whose rules I hadn't learned well. It was demoralising and an expensive education. I came close to bankruptcy but avoided it by the grace of God. It certainly contributed to the breakdown of my first marriage.

Now, on the other side of that painful experience, I'd say it was the best lesson I ever learned in business. Sure, I had to lick my wounds for a while. Then I decided I'd never go into business again. I retreated to senior finance positions, first with a successful meat exporter, next with the country's largest privately-owned car and truck tyre importer, then in the nation's second largest mental health organisation.

They all taught me valuable lessons; but try as I might, I couldn't shake off my love for business. Somehow, I just had to keep progressing that dream. I continued to ask every question I could think of, to understand what makes a business successful. Why did some work and others fail?

In 2017 I was taken by surprise when God called me, unambiguously, to start an advisory business to help other Small and Medium Enterprise businesses (SMEs) improve their operations, profits, and values. To be honest, I laughed! "Really?" I thought. "Who'd take advice from a 'serial business failure'?" (which is how I thought of myself, forgetting for a time just how much I'd learned through all those experiences). But, as I inched forward towards this unexpected call, I discovered God had a radical new plan for me, and for my future clients.

When God calls, everything changes. I joined a consultancy company, which was part of an ex-franchise collective called *The Consulting Group*, covering all of New Zealand. To my astonishment, my performance pushed me to second place nationwide in just six months, then first place 18 months later, remaining there for the life of the group.

What made that difference?

Nearly five years ago, I was introduced to business from a new, Kingdom-of-God-centred, perspective. A radically new way of helping every business that became my client. Most of my clients weren't followers of Jesus – but I was. God blessed them as we worked together. Not one business I worked with during my four years with *The Consulting Group*, has closed its doors as a result of the Covid-19 epidemic. Many improved significantly.

Chapter 1 describes how this change came about.

This book will have done its job if, as you read, you keep encountering the risen Jesus – not primarily in my words, but in every page of the Bible, from which this book's insights have been mined. Jesus reveals Himself not as a moraliser nor philosopher, but as your living, vibrant, thought-provoking, attractive Lord and Friend – the best One you'll ever have. (Re)discover His restoring presence, and His unlimited participation in everything you're involved with in life, including your business.

I pray you'll see the joy and freedom that comes from surrendering everything to Him; allowing Him to shower you with the blessings of His Kingdom, as He has for me, and countless others.

He does so only on His terms. We can never separate the King from the Kingdom. But by embracing the King's invitation His way, then:

> *...no matter how many promises God has made, they are "Yes" in Christ.* (2 Cor. 1:20a, NIV).

Enjoy, and be blessed!

CHAPTER 1
"WHAT IF YOU MAKE GOD YOUR CEO?"

"I am the Lord; I will bring you out from under the burdens of the Egyptians, I will rescue you from their bondage, and I will redeem you with an outstretched arm and with great judgments."
(Exo. 6:6, NKJV).

"For I am the LORD your God who takes hold of your right hand and says to you, 'Do not fear, I will help you'."
(Isa. 41:13, NIV).

In April 2017, an 80+ year old friend and prayer-mentor of mine – a loyal intercessor who'd stood in the gap (see Eze. 22:30) for me over many years – asked me one question that sent a tidal wave crashing into my mind. It caused a paradigm shift so dramatic that, within moments of him asking me, everything altered in my head.

I'd just said to him: "I'm so grateful for the extended time I've had with God over the past year, slowing down the pace of my life and deepening my relationship with Him so measurably. As I start my new business, I'd love you to continue praying for me, so I don't lose that depth of connection to Him."

That sounded to me like a good observation — something which I hoped would draw out his empathy and encourage him to keep praying for me. Instead, he looked me straight in the eye and said, "That's the wrong comment!"

To be honest, I was rattled. He certainly had my attention. I searched my mind trying to understand what I'd said that he thought was so out of place. In the end I had to concede — "Tell me, what have I said that's wrong?"

His reply was my game-changer: "Peter. What if it's not *your* business? What if you make God your CEO and you become nothing more than His employee?"

It was like an instantaneous mental earthquake! Suddenly I realised — no, I *saw* — that we are never called to live *for* God — He calls us to live *with* Him . . . and that difference is enormous. I'd never again have to shoulder problems alone or suffer sleepless nights due to stress. Responsibility had shifted.

Being a father myself, I'd already heard God tell me that He will take care of my children: He's a better Father than I'll ever be. Yes, I'd heard, and responded to, that invitation to let Him lead my family . . . But my business? It had never occurred to me that He could — *and wants to* — lead our businesses too, practically, operationally, day-to-day.

For the past five years, I've been learning excitedly, and encouraging anyone who'll accept the challenge, to adopt Him as their CEO too. What you're reading is one result of that life-changing moment and God's subsequent mentoring of me, through His Word, His Spirit, and the wise input of fellow disciples.

The Bible refers to Him as Lord or King. The CEO is the equivalent role in business. The two chapter title verses indicate that, as our CEO (Lord) He promises to bring us out from under burdens, rescue us from becoming oppressed by any circumstances or people within our businesses, support us when others are against us, grab our hands when they fail, and be our ever present help (see Psa. 46:1) – all the time encouraging us not to be afraid but to trust Him, in faith.

That's quite a way in which to start, or lead, a business! I trust that you will find Him in all those ways, and more, as you read on.

CHAPTER 2
FAITH ISN'T OPTIONAL!

But without faith, it is impossible to please Him, for he who comes to God must believe that He is, and that He is a rewarder of those who diligently seek Him.
(Heb. 11:6, NKJV).

And the apostles said to the Lord, "Increase our faith." So the Lord said, "If you have faith as a mustard seed, you can say to this mulberry tree, 'Be pulled up by the roots and be planted in the sea,' and it would obey you."
(Luke 17:5-6, NKJV).

Have you noticed that, often, the statements of Jesus[1] leave no wriggle-room?

He was not offering a new "Law" under which He intended to analyse us dispassionately from a distance, demanding we conform or else be judged. No! His deep and enduring passion is an *intimate relationship with His people*.

---

[1] Recorded by multiple eyewitnesses, in the books of the New Testament.

We live through faith. We're saved through faith. We work through faith. We obey through faith. Without faith it's not possible to please Him.

Without embracing the depth of relationship He offers us, and stepping out in faith with Him, it's impossible to do any of the things He tells us we can do (see Matt. 10:8). We may be believers in Jesus, yet not followers. We may be moral but not life-giving. Or saved but not fruitful.

This is uncomfortable, because there's no formula for living a life of faith; no Standard Operating Procedures we can tick off, proving "job done". There's only a restored relationship (see John 17:21).

And that restoration invites us to a journey of personal transformation – of us and our businesses.

> **This invitation is to *know* Him – to 'fellowship' with God – intimately.**

Therefore, whilst we can look forward to growing successful businesses, our starting point isn't going to be either capitalist or commercial models, both of which are society's set-ups, not God's. I'd like to introduce you to another approach altogether – a possibility and opportunity which dares to take God at His Word, letting Him be – genuinely, extraordinarily – *the CEO of our businesses.*

It starts with faith. Since He says we *must* have faith (see Heb. 11:6), doesn't this suggest to you that there's something on God's mind far more exciting, dynamic, world-changing, than a mere commercial enterprise into which we sprinkle Christian values, morals, or ethics in an attempt to demonstrate its difference? Could there, instead, be a truly sensational, alternative journey offered to us?

I believe, with all my heart: Yes! It's a journey of faith.

I don't mean pie-in-the-sky ideology. I mean:

- practically, strategically and operationally embracing God's work *in* our businesses,
- furthering the purposes of *His* Kingdom,
- transforming the world around us, and
- glorifying His Son.

In short, fulfilling the Great Commission (see Matt. 28:18-20). It means that our businesses are no longer simply vehicles to *fund* missions – they *become* the mission: a vehicle by which God is revealed to the world.

Persistently and consistently the God of the Bible has expected His children to live by a completely different foundation, compared to the yardsticks used by society in general. We are to be a revelation of Him so attractive to the world, that all people are drawn to Jesus (see John 12:32). He invites us to do what is impossible without Him; then empowers us to do it. Starting with Adam, Noah, and Abram (Abraham), He has never deviated from this faith-demanding strategy; not in thousands of years of interactions between the Trinity and mankind.

What, then, is our part?

> ***Jesus answered and said to them, "This is the work of God, that you believe in Him whom He sent." (John 6:29, NKJV).***

Likewise, Paul talked about *the obedience of faith* (Rom 1:5, NASB). Not 'obedience *and* faith' as if they were separate, but 'the obedience *of* faith'.

How can such a thing be? Where do we start?

Let's remember what Jesus told us, about how fruitfulness is produced in our lives.

> *"Abide in Me, and I in you. As the branch cannot bear fruit of itself, unless it abides in the vine, neither can you, unless you abide in Me."* (John 15:4, NKJV).

There is no other way but the development of a relationship with Him, so deep, personal, and obedient, that we welcome Him living His life through us, even passing His desires onto us so that we want what He wants. Just three verses further on, He repeats Himself, but with a twist that indicates the promise He's extending to us:

> *If you abide in Me, and My words abide in you, you will ask what you desire, and it shall be done for you. By this My Father is glorified, that you bear much fruit; so you will be My disciples.* (John 15:7-8, NKJV).

With so much promise and adventure at stake, why is it so hard for us to take the first step, following Him into the unknown?

Perhaps simply because it *is* unknown. Who knows where He will lead? Yet, I think that's the whole point. Faith isn't faith if we already know exactly what's going to happen, right?

Faith, by its nature, demands trust – trust in a Person (see Rom. 10:17; John 1:1,14). As our relationship with that Person grows, faith grows also, becoming strong enough to trust Him, wherever He may call us.

Are you willing to embark – to quantify the risk and see where this journey of faith might lead? It is the gentle tug of His Spirit, "Come walk with Me". And He is faithful. He even adds a promise never to abandon us or let us down. We can be absolutely certain of His dependability, as we commit to walk with Him.

> *For He Himself has said, "I will never leave you nor forsake you."* (Heb. 13:5b, NKJV).
> (See also Gen. 28:15; Deut. 31:6; Josh. 1:5; and Matt. 28:20b).

Not that everything will always be rosy – I don't mean that. In fact, it's entirely likely He'll ask us to go through dark and difficult experiences, perhaps often. Faith is formed in the crucible, not on the couch. But when He does, bank on this: even there, we'll find His faithful presence. We'll be able to echo the words of David with confidence:

> *...though I walk through the valley of the shadow of death, I fear no evil; for You are with me; Your rod and Your staff, they comfort me.* (Psa. 23:4, NKJV).

A final word before we move on:

Faith doesn't always remove fear or doubt. Neither do fear or doubt invalidate faith in any way.[2] Faith isn't a feeling: it's

---

[2] In fact, the antidote to fear isn't faith, it's love (see 1 John 4:18).

a gift (see Eph. 2:8). It's the evidence of things we hope and pray for, that haven't yet shown up in physical form (see Heb. 11:1).[3] Sometimes we have no option but to operate in faith whilst feeling afraid — or overwhelmed, or a raft of other emotions too (see Neh. 2:1-3 and Mark 9:24, for examples). Don't let anyone tell you that your emotions disqualify you from faith, or any other of the gifts God gives to you. That's deception — and we all know where that comes from!

So, with that said, if you're ready for a challenge — the sometimes uncomfortable but always rewarding, boundary-expanding adventure of faith — let's begin!

---

[3] From a Biblical perspective, 'seeing isn't believing'. Rather, 'believing is seeing' (see Heb. 11:1)

CHAPTER 3
THE CALL (EXCITING - BUT BEWARE TOO!)

> *...one thing I do, forgetting those things which are behind and reaching forward to those things which are ahead, I press toward the goal for the prize of the upward call of God in Christ Jesus.*
>
> (Phil. 3:13b-14, NKJV).

The reasons people start businesses are almost as numerous as the people who do so. For instance:

- The independence of not being under someone else's beck and call.
- To gain hoped-for control over our own lives.
- Wanting more time – or more control over our time.
- We have a great idea and are keen to give it a go, to see if we can make it work.
- We're motivated by an infectious enthusiasm that somehow tells us that we *know* we'll do better if we work for ourselves.
- We're motivated by money, or a social vision, or we want to prove to ourselves the validity of the American Dream ideology.
- We may consider it a simple necessity, when all other avenues close (and we've been seeing this during the

Covid pandemic, as people have lost jobs and can't find others).

I'd like to throw another reason at you, which perhaps you've never considered:-

> **As a Christian business owner, you're *called* into business, by God.[4]**

Every believer who wishes to take seriously the life of faith, is subject to the same, simple, universal, call that Jesus issued to His disciples: *"Follow Me"!* It's a call to walk *with* Him!

When we do so, He said we'd do the very same things He did (see John 14:12).

That's not your idea, it's His. He never asked you to run a business *for* Him; He invited you to run it *with* Him.

Our problem is that we default to working *for* God. Why? Perhaps because our relationship with Him isn't intimate enough to trust Him to that extent, or perhaps we've never even thought of doing so. In either case, we're reduced to a reliance on our own experience and education, formal or informal, to be our fall-back position. I'm not saying that God doesn't use skills, knowledge, wisdom, learned abilities and gifts; He created those too, and He does (see Exo. 31:3). But Zechariah the prophet was clear that such an approach to fulfilling our calling in Him, isn't God's intention:

---

[4] Actually there is another alternative to consider for some...that you *haven't* been called into business at all – it was all your own idea. In this case, both the evidence of your eyes, and the words of your friends will readily reveal it to you, and you should probably get out of business a.s.a.p., before you find yourself deeply discouraged.

"Not by might, nor by power, but by My Spirit," says the Lord of hosts. (Zech. 4:6, NKJV).

What does "following Jesus" look like in business?

Together, we'll unpack that, not least through the stories of others. But let's begin by reminding ourselves that it's not about 'rule-keeping' where, if we slip up, we will be scolded and blamed.[5] Rather, it's about grasping the extraordinary opportunity extended to us in Jesus' invitation to get to know Him so well, that we can follow His *life*, not just His example.

> 'Following Jesus' is a call that is both invitational and incarnational.

If we're genuinely going to follow Jesus, it shouldn't be any surprise that we'll experience, in our call to entrepreneurship, the same hallmarks that exist in any and every call of God.

Furthermore, every call will leave you exposed. As one contributor to this book, Tracey Olivier, an entrepreneur herself, said to me: "I often tell budding entrepreneurs: If you really want to know what your weaknesses, failings and emotional triggers are, go into business!"[6]

So let me share with you nine hallmarks of every call of God – experienced by Jesus also:-

---

[5] That's satan's strategy, not God's (see Rev.12:10)

[6] Tracey's contact details are given in chapter 13, where she has kindly contributed some Entrepreneur's Insights.

1) Evidence

> *The One who calls you is faithful, and He will do it.* (1 Thess. 5:24, NIV).

There is always an 'inner witness' to you personally, which also is – or becomes – obvious and corroborated by others: they will be able to confirm it with you. Calls recorded in the Bible were evidenced by way of:

- The inner voice of the Holy Spirit (e.g. Abraham, in Gen. 12:1)
- Visions (e.g. Abraham and Paul, in Gen. 15:1-6 and Acts 9:3-6)
- Dreams (e.g. Joseph and Paul, in Gen. 37:5-11 and Acts 16:9)
- Prophetic anointing (e.g. both Saul and David, in 1 Sam. 10:1 and 1 Sam. 16:13)
- Circumstances and opportunity (e.g. Rahab and Daniel, in Josh. 2:14 and Dan. 1:8-17)
- Angel visits (e.g. Zacharias, Mary and Joseph, in Luke 1:5-20, Luke 1:26-38, and Matt. 1:18-21)
- The laying on of hands (e.g. Timothy, in 1 Tim. 4:14)

The call of Jesus Himself was attested in all these ways, as well as being both announced and evidenced all the way through Scripture, from Genesis to Revelation.

2) Faith

> *But someone will say, "You have faith, and I have works." Show me your faith without your works, and I will show you my faith by my works.* (Jam. 2:18, NKJV).

Faith must always be *applied* faith. Not actioned out of presumption; only those actions asked of us by Jesus. If nothing is required of us for a season, it's wise to ask God whether we've missed some opportunity to exercise faith in Him, or whether we're in a time of rest, a lull in His proceedings – in which case, enjoy it!

There are always uncomfortable things asked of us in business, by God. He chooses, in His grace, to make sure we haven't resumed control of His enterprise. Also, that it hasn't taken over control of us, occupying the place in our hearts that's reserved for Him alone.

He asks us to hold His work lightly, operating it as stewards for Him, so that it can fulfil His purpose, not primarily our own. Yet grace is evidenced in a spill-over effect, by which we, too, are blessed and fulfilled, as we obey Him.

3) **Brokenness**

> *And the Lord turned and looked at Peter. Then Peter remembered the word of the Lord, how He had said to him, "Before the rooster crows, you will deny Me three times."* (Luke 22:61, NKJV).

Oh, don't we hate it when our apparent failures are put on public display – especially when they're a result of our own stupid actions? Doesn't it make us squirm? Yet through it, our egos are humbled, and we surrender more deeply to the generosity of His Lordship.

There was no visible glory in Christ's death on the Cross. Rather, it was His vulnerability and brokenness through which God revealed glory, victory and love. His brokenness was committed to public record for all time in the Gospels, both in the Garden of Gethsemane (e.g. Luke 22:39-44) and on the Cross (e.g. Matt. 27:26-35). How then can we think we might avoid brokenness?

- Joseph was stripped, thrown into a pit, then sold into slavery (see Gen. 37:23-28).
- David's life was threatened multiple times, forcing him to act mad and live as an outcast for years (see 1 Sam. 21:10-15; 24:1-15).
- Daniel was made a slave, likely castrated (see Dan. 1:8, NKJV, ESV, AMPC), then thrown to lions (see Dan. 6:16-17).
- Peter was denounced by Jesus in front of his peers (see Matt 16:23), then later denied Jesus – not once but three times! (see Mark 14:66-72).

All four of these men had either been in business or were called to serve God through business positions. Their brokenness became the catalyst through which God released significant blessings, not only in their personal lives but into and through their working lives also.

What if we were to see brokenness as a blessing, bringing life to us and others, and giving glory to Christ?

4) <u>Surrender</u>

> *"...those of you who do not give up everything you have, cannot be my disciples."* (Luke 14:33, NIV).

Jesus is uncompromising. Discipleship – following Him – can't be achieved by putting ourselves in first place.

We're not the master, and He's not Santa, handing out sweets/candies of success — financial or otherwise. We must travel the way He walked — the Way that He *is* (see John 14:6).[7]

Although some blessings are available for all mankind, indiscriminately (see Matt. 5:45), there are some entrusted to us only after surrender.[8] Not as rewards for good behaviour or evidence of His endorsement, but simply because He's decided there is no other way (see John 12:24).

Surrender is to allow God to take up His rightful place in our lives and businesses — as King, Lord, Master, CEO. Under His leadership we, and our businesses, prosper.[9] If instead, we are determined to operate our businesses under our own control, they become games of Russian roulette, subject to the vagaries of our own skills,

---

[7] It's because of these and many other similar words of Jesus (alongside the example of His own life), that make it impossible for me to embrace the so-called 'faith gospel' or 'prosperity gospel', both of which want to bypass the Cross and instead head straight for the 'cookie jar' of soft-option blessings. In doing so they ignore the fullness of the gospel, which requires sacrifice, obedience and surrender to the will of God:
Faith's initial job is to lead us to Salvation (Eph. 2:8); => Salvation leads us into deeper relationship with Jesus (John 15:4); => Jesus leads us to take up our Cross (Matt. 16:24); => The Cross leads us to Surrender (1 Peter 5:6); => Surrender leads to Obedience (Phil 2:5-11); => Obedience opens the way for blessing (1 Peter 3:9).

[8] Meaning a 'death' to self-centredness.

[9] Meaning far more than mere accumulation of wealth or money. It's about the Abundant Life that Jesus declared as His longing for us (John 10:10) — encompassing absolutely every area of our lives, including our businesses. It embraces 'all of life restoration and wholeness'.

abilities, gifts, market conditions, etc. We will never access the immense resources available to us in the Kingdom of God that way. Tragedy!

5) Obedience...

> *Jesus replied, "Anyone who loves Me will obey My teaching."* (John 14:23, NIV).

> *Though He was a Son, yet He learned obedience by the things which He suffered.* (Heb. 5:8, NKJV).

Obedience isn't optional. It's an inevitable outcome of our faith in Him — and evidence of it. No one is immune, not even Christ Himself.

This isn't slave-like, dutiful obedience. It's willing submission, borne of utmost respect, to the One who always has our best interests at heart. It isn't arduous, nor a yoke around our necks. It's a sheer delight, leading to untold favour and blessing:-

> *...looking unto Jesus, the author and finisher of our faith, who for the joy that was set before Him endured the cross, despising the shame, and has sat down at the right hand of the throne of God.* (Heb 12:2, NKJV).

6) ...to the point of Sacrifice

> *"Whoever wants to be My disciple must deny themselves and take up their Cross daily and follow Me."* (Luke 9:23, NIV).

> *So Jesus answered and said, "Assuredly, I say to you, there is no one who has left house or brothers or sisters or father or mother or wife or children or lands, for My sake and the gospel's, who shall not receive a hundredfold now in this time—houses and brothers and sisters and mothers and children and lands, with persecutions—and in the age to come, eternal life."* (Mark 10:29-30, NKJV).

Sacrifice and obedience are linked. We're asked to sacrifice everything to Him so that He, in return, can display the lavishness of His grace to us. This is His character! He *loves* to bless in extravagant abundance[10], *far* beyond our own expectations for ourselves.

He asks us: "Do you *really* want to keep a foot in both camps, trying to serve Me as well as gain the world? (Matt. 16:26). Or are you willing to lay down everything, including your family, your life, and your business?"

> *Most assuredly, I say to you, unless a grain of wheat falls into the ground and dies, it remains alone; but if it dies, it produces much grain.* (John 12:24, NKJV).

7) <u>Holiness</u>

> *"Be holy because I, the Lord your God, am holy."* (Lev. 19:2, NIV).

---

[10] Note, though, that our understanding of what God considers to be a 'blessing' may need to change. Did you notice that persecution is on the list too – both in these verses and, even more directly, in the Sermon on the Mount (see Matt 5:11)?

Yes – as a businessperson! Holiness isn't just for church pastors and ministers. Like everything God asks us to do, we can't achieve it on our own. It must be by faith.

We're totally reliant on the power of Holy Spirit within us, for the development of His character within us. Failure to recognise that a holy life is preferable to one in which we excuse and perpetuate our sins, can affect our business significantly – far more than we would wish to admit.

The reason God invites us to align our lives with His life of obedience, power and resurrection, is so we may then live under the astonishing blessings that come from such holiness. As before, it's the things we do *with* Him, not *for* Him, that give Him – and us – untold pleasure.

Will you accept His call to holiness? I've seen this transform businesses radically.

8) Character Development (evidenced!)

> *For this very reason, make every effort to add to your faith goodness; and to goodness, knowledge; and to knowledge, self-control; and to self-control, perseverance; and to perseverance, godliness; and to godliness, mutual affection; and to mutual affection, love. For if you possess these qualities in increasing measure, they will keep you from being ineffective and unproductive in your knowledge of our Lord Jesus Christ.* (2 Pet. 1:5-8, NIV).

> *Get wisdom. Though it cost all you have, get understanding. Cherish her, and she will exalt*

you; embrace her, and she will honour you. She will give you a garland to grace your head and present you with a glorious crown. (Prov. 4:7b-9, NIV).

Owning a business *will* expose our emotional immaturity and flawed characters – guaranteed! For instance –

- fear, anger, insecurity, sarcasm,
- a 'need' to be in control,
- a lack of identity,
- feelings of rejection,
- pettiness,
- lack of resilience,
- a failure to endure,
- inability to accept criticism, allowing customer service to suffer because we've taken the huff.

Being tested in all of these areas is simply par for the course in business.

My heartfelt plea is this: Get whatever help you need, to defuse emotional 'bombs' before they emerge – because they will if they're there. Hidden, damaging emotions that become exposed unexpectedly, can sabotage your business.

9) Evidence of Miracles

When [Jesus] had stopped speaking, He said to Simon, "Launch out into the deep and let down your nets for a catch." But Simon answered and said to Him, "Master, we have toiled all night and caught nothing; nevertheless

> *at Your word I will let down the net." And when they had done this, they caught a great number of fish, and their net was breaking. So they signalled to their partners in the other boat to come and help them. And they came and filled both the boats, so that they began to sink. When Simon Peter saw it, he fell down at Jesus' knees, saying, "Depart from me, for I am a sinful man, O Lord!"* (Luke 5:4-8, NKJV).

> *"Most assuredly, I say to you, he who believes in Me, the works that I do he will do also; and greater works than these he will do, because I go to My Father."* (John 14:12, NKJV).

Whenever ancient Israel went into battle, if they consulted God first, He always gave them a strategy that ensured a successful outcome. This success was evidence that they'd chosen humility — intentional dependence on Him — through the exercise of faith. God fulfilled miraculous outcomes on their behalf.[11] (We'll explore this further in Chapter 4).

He loves to surprise and to bless us with unexpected and impossible outcomes! Let this wonderful aspect of your call in Christ take its place in your business.

---

[11] They could understandably have arrived at the conclusion that they were such seasoned fighters, they knew all the military strategies that should be followed. When they took that approach, disastrous defeats were *always* the outcome (see, e.g., Lev. 26:14,17; Num. 21:1; Deut. 28:15,25; 1 Sam. 4:10).

So, a question before we move on:

> **Have *you* heard, clearly and discernibly,
> God's call over your life, in business?**

If not, may I encourage you to spend time with Him now – as long as it takes – to hear Him[12] and receive clarity about your call into business, before you read further? You could use questions, such as:

- Am I confident that He does intend me to be in business?
- How is that confidence made clear to me?
- Can others confirm it?
- Am I willing to spend time seeking Him each day, for His (not my) successful outcomes in the business?
- What are they? – What's His Overall Purpose for the business He's called me to start?
- How will I know (and make sure) I'm continuing to fulfil that purpose faithfully?
- How do I/will I handle things, when they go wrong?
- How do I/will I handle things when they go right?
- Am I willing to let Him take the lead and show me the way? – to make Him my CEO?
- What difference will that make to any other model of business I've previously held true?

---

[12] If you aren't sure how to hear God's voice, see the suggestions, at the end of this book, for *Further Reading,* Mark & Patti Virkler's book *4 Keys to Hearing God's Voice.* It's a very good, and practical, guide grounded in Scripture.

If, however, you answered yes (and discerning others confirm it), you could still ask further questions, such as:

- Is God truly my CEO, or am I still trying to take charge?
- Am I remaining vulnerable and dependent on Him all the time?
- Do I *"pray without ceasing"*, as I go about God's work? **(1 Thess. 5:17, NKJV)**
- Is there a risk I feel I've learned how the business works? Am I continuing what He started, in my own strength doing it without Him? How will I change that?
- What evidence is there, in both my life and business, of the nine features of every call? Do I need to alter course with Him? If so, what will I do about that?
- Is my business operating with a Kingdom focus? If not, how can it?

Either way, allow me to encourage you: *Once you've started with Him, never stop surrendering or listening to Him.* One church in the New Testament did, and the severity with which Paul wrote to them was not pretty –

> *Are you so foolish? After beginning by means of the Spirit, are you now trying to finish by means of the flesh?* (Gal. 3:3, NIV).

Instead, allow God free rein to take control over all aspects of your business:

> *But the natural man does not receive the things of the Spirit of God, for they are foolishness to him; nor can he know them, because they are spiritually discerned... But we have the mind of Christ.* (1 Cor. 2:14,16b, NKJV).

CHAPTER 4
THE CENTRALITY OF THE KINGDOM

> *Now when He was asked by the Pharisees when the Kingdom of God would come, He answered them and said, "The Kingdom of God does not come with observation; nor will they say, 'See here!' or 'See there!' For indeed, the Kingdom of God is within you."*
>
> (Luke 17:20-21, NKJV).

Rather than attempt a comprehensive theology of 'The Kingdom of God', I prefer Jesus' approach to complex issues: He simplified them for us. My intention is that we hear what's at stake.

So my simple, workable explanation is:-

The Kingdom of God is where Jesus reigns.

The key 'place' in which the Kingdom of God is evidenced, is in human hearts – our hearts. God gives us a choice: will we, or won't we, accept His all-embracing Lordship? When you or I allow Jesus to be our King we become subjects in His Kingdom. We acknowledge His right to rule over us. His Kingdom is evidenced in us. In business, we'd call Him our CEO.

And as we embrace His gracious rule, surrendering willingly to it, the blessings of His Kingdom become immediately and abundantly available to us.

> *I have come that they may have life, and that they may have it more abundantly.* (John 10:10b, NKJV).

> *And all these blessings shall come upon you and overtake you if you obey the Lord your God . . .* (Deut. 28:2, NASB 1995).

As we express His Kingship into the world, all of creation is aligned with His beautiful plan: to reconcile and restore all things – including humanity – into a restored relationship with Him:

> *For God was pleased to have all His fullness dwell in Him, and through Him to reconcile to Himself all things, whether things on earth or things in heaven, by making peace through His blood, shed on the cross.* (Col. 1:19-20, NIV).

Since His Kingdom is within us then, by extension, it must be –

- ✓ in every prayer we pray,
- ✓ in everything we do,
- ✓ in everything we touch,
- ✓ in every relationship we have,
- ✓ in every business we operate.

Is it beginning to make sense now, why acknowledging God as our CEO is so important?

- It's a matter of us living in His Kingdom, and letting Him express Himself through us and our businesses, into the world.
- It's about a business being far more than a societal, socialist or capitalist model of generating profit for shareholders or stakeholders.
- It's far more than the business merely supporting us and our families, or the families of our employees and suppliers and customers.
- It's far more than a business offering products and services, to serve the world.

> Business is an opportunity to work alongside the King, expressing His Kingship on earth, through what He's asked us to build and steward on His behalf.

Kingdom Business

A Kingdom business, therefore, is a business that operates from a very different foundation – a foundation of Jesus Himself. It's resourced and enabled by His Life, His power, His authority, His creativity, His ability to affect and change every aspect of the world around Him. And He administers all of this through us.[13]

---

[13] Note: All of these resources remain His. We aren't supposed to remove them out of His hands, using His gifts without Him being present. We're to remain integrally dependant on Him, for all time. Our businesses become His businesses, so they demonstrate His love, compassion, life, and freedom to a world that so desperately needs Him – whether they recognise Him or not.

Just to be clear, I *don't* mean –

- turn your business into a 'religious' organisation, nor
- employ only Christians, nor
- become a religious zealot, nor
- shove the gospel at people for no better reason than because they breathe!

I mean it's about –

- your life with God, and how you allow Him to live with you, in your business;
- your surrender to God, and how you apply that in business;
- your obedience to God, and how you follow Him in business;
- your willingness to receive God's supernatural leading, power and enabling; and
- your asking for His strategies then, as you hear and apply them, watching His results unfold – bringing glory to Jesus so He becomes evident to a watching world.

Larry Julian, in his book[14], includes the following table, which contrasts the Unwritten Business Rules of general, commercial business, with God's Principles. It's a wonderful summary of juxtaposition, and explains why Christians can have genuine challenges in undertaking commercial activities using society's rules:-

---

[14] *God is my CEO: Following God's Principles in a Bottom-Line World*, 2nd Edition, by Larry Julian, Copyright © 2014, 2002, 2001 by Larry S. Julian, p. xix (Introduction), Reprinted with permission of the Publisher, Adams Media, an imprint of Simon & Schuster, Inc. All rights reserved.

Business Principles versus God's Principles	
Unwritten Business Rules	God's Principles
• Achieve results	• Serve a purpose
• What can I get?	• How can I give?
• Success = dollars	• Significance = people
• Work to please people	• Work to please God
• Fear of the unknown	• Living with hope
• Leadership is being first	• Leadership is being last
• Take charge; surrender means defeat	• Let go; surrender means victory
• The end justifies the means. Get to the outcome regardless of how you accomplish it.	• The means justifies the end. Do the right thing regardless of the outcome.
• Short-term gain	• Long-term legacy
• Slave to the urgent	• Freedom of choice
• You can never produce enough	• Unconditional love

I love his astuteness!

It leads to a very important question: 'Can these differences be reconciled?'

A blunt appraisal shows that, without a lot of squeezing, they can't – much as we might like that not to be our answer. And many of us have neither recognised it, nor looked before at the implications.[15]

However, they *can* co-exist.

When we grasp what a God-centred business looks like, viewed through the lens of Jesus' own mission, we can forge a new and different path into commerce, where businesses *are* the expression of His mission; they don't merely fund missions. We start not from the perspective of, 'How do I make a business venture successful?' but rather, 'What does it look like to follow Jesus in business?'

---

[15] Let's look at just one from his table, by way of example:-
Success focuses on *specific actions* needed to generate financial attainment and business growth.
- *Its features* are material and financial outcomes.
- *Its measures* are KPI's.
- *Profit* is always the target.

Whereas **significance** focuses on *individuals and their characters*, to fulfil and achieve God's mission.
- *Its features* are a surrendered life, faith, servanthood and obedience.
- *Its measure* is the fruit of the Spirit.
- *Profit* is never the target; rather that's an outcome for which God takes responsibility; and it's an inevitability whilst the business continues to fulfil Jesus' Kingdom purposes (see Deut. 8:18; Phil. 4:19).

Kingdom businesses aren't just 'commercial enterprises with Christian values added'; they are (through God's invitation and our surrender) expressions of His life and light into a commercial world. As Paul put it:-

> *For you were once darkness, but now you are light in the Lord. Walk as children of light.* (Eph. 5:8, NKJV).

The prophet Micah clarifies some specifics – applicable to business, as well as life in general:

> *He has shown you, O man, what is good; and what does the Lord require of you but to do justly, to love mercy, and to walk humbly with your God?* (Micah 6:8, NKJV).

Just to be clear, I'm not suggesting a wholesale abandonment of anything and everything that commercial business looks like. But I am suggesting that the foundations of a God-centric, Christ-following, Kingdom-surrendered business, do need to be completely different. For that reason, for the time being, we do need

- to set aside every commercial business practice, whilst we
- re-write the foundations of business, based on the life and practice of Jesus. Only then
- can we review what we set aside, to see what, and how much, of the world's lessons can be valuably embraced into a business where Jesus is at the head as its CEO.

His Kingdom is Absurdly Different!

If you know your Scriptures, you'll know that God's Kingdom is wildly different from anything society expects it to be – to the point of offending those who perceive themselves as wise. As Paul put it:-

> *But God chose the foolish things of the world to shame the wise; God chose the weak things of the world to shame the strong.* (1 Cor. 1:27, NIV).

Even His plans are different! If you're still used to working *for* Him, you'll still be setting up your own plans and asking Him to bless them. Whereas, when we work *with* Him, our businesses need to operate with the plans He sets for them – even when He shares only the smallest portion of them at a time (see Gen. 12:1); because our call is to operate by faith, not by sight.

> *A man's heart plans his way, but the Lord directs his steps.* (Prov. 16:9, NKJV).

Consider, for example, the strategic plans that God gave the ancient Israelites, to defeat their enemies. Each battle plan was totally different from every other. There was no One Winning Plan.

Yet there was an overarching Strategy – namely, to *ask God, listen, hear, then obey what He told them to do*. That was it! Yes, each plan seemed outlandish; yet they enacted it, confident in His faithfulness . . . and God honoured His word.

Here is a sample:-

1. Send out spies, before engaging the enemy (Num. 13);
2. Walk around Jericho in silence 13 times total, then shout on the 14th (Josh. 6);
3. Engage in normal, military combat, but with God making the sun stand still, so they could finish the battle (Josh. 10);
4. Paring back the army from 22,000 to just 300, before facing the enemy – and then, only with trumpets, torches and jars (Judg. 7);
5. Send just Jonathan and his armour-bearer to rout the army alone (1 Sam. 14:1-23);
6. Circle around behind, then wait before striking, until they heard marching in the tree tops (2 Sam. 5);
7. Send singers out in front of the army. Don't fight – I'll fight for you (2 Chr. 20).

Can God still deliver like this today? I wonder how we'll fare, as strategies like this are given us.

If your business is going to express the fullness of His Kingdom – and experience the blessings available through it – we need to be clear about what that means. So, the rest of this book will focus on some specific attributes of the Kingdom, examining each from a Biblical perspective, and applying them into the business context. You'll meet different business owners in each chapter, who have offered their experiences and generously given me permission to tell their stories; along with one or two of my own. In doing so, I hope you'll gain a refreshed, new and/or deeper understanding of what's available to your business, in Christ; and of His love and invitation, extended to you.

These are the characteristics of God's Kingdom we'll look at. The Kingdom is —

- *Already Established;*
- *Identity-Giving;*
- *Outrageous;*
- *Attractive;*
- *Upside-Down;*
- *Forgiving;*
- *Sacrificial;*
- *Holy;*
- *Abundant;*
- *Transforming;*
- *Resourcing;*
- *Unlimited;*
- *Miraculous;*
- *Embracing.*

I pray that, as you read, you'll begin a journey of receiving, by faith, every blessing God intends both for you and your business, as you build it on these Kingdom qualities. More than that, *as you build on the very foundation of Jesus Himself,* whose power is available to us — to you — through the incarnation, birth, life, death, resurrection, ascension, glorification and enthronement of Jesus:

> **Now to Him who is able to do exceedingly abundantly above all that we ask or think, according to the power that works in us, to Him be glory in the church by Christ Jesus to all generations, forever and ever. Amen. (Eph. 3:20-21, NKJV).**

His stated intent (see also John 10:10) is to prosper you in the widest possible meaning of that word – and through you, your business – so that we express whole-of-life riches and abundance, without them holding us in their thrall. Because everything is for the praise of His glory.

CHAPTER 5
THE GOD-ESTABLISHED BUSINESS

> *Lord, You have searched me and known me. You know when I sit down and when I get up; You understand my thought from far away. You scrutinize my path and my lying down, and are acquainted with all my ways. Even before there is a word on my tongue, behold, Lord, You know it all. You have encircled me behind and in front, and placed Your hand upon me. Such knowledge is too wonderful for me; it is too high, I cannot comprehend it.*
> (Psa. 139:1-6, NASB).

One of the neatest things about being a Christian in business, is that the end is known from before we start – at least to God! This isn't surprising, really, since:

> *"I am the Alpha and the Omega, the Beginning and the End, the First and the Last."* (Rev. 22:13, NKJV).

Everything God does is good. And complete.

Before He began creation, His purpose, intentions, and plans were already formed. So, by the time He came to act, He simply spoke and it was so (Gen. 1:1 – 2:3). Over and over again, God poured out His creative personality into the universe, in words (actually, *as* the Word – John 1:1-3); and all physical matter, including that which hadn't existed before He began to speak, obeyed His exact expectations.

Business implications and application

In grasping this, we get a totally different picture of how we can operate in our businesses. We're on a journey not to *create* a business; but rather to *discover* one. God has already gone ahead of us. Our job is to understand *His* purpose, not generate our own. We pray, wait, watch, listen (see Psa. 46:10 and John 15:7-8) – and only act when He speaks, giving us the next move –

> *"Truly, truly, I say to you, the Son can do nothing of Himself, unless it is something He sees the Father doing; for whatever the Father does, these things the Son also does in the same way."* (John 5:19, NASB);

– and

> *"Truly, truly I say to you, the one who believes in Me, the works that I do, he will do also; and greater works than these he will do; because I am going to the Father."* (John 14:12, NASB).

Thus, our businesses, being part of our lives, are God-inspired, God-initiated, and God-purposed.

But there's even more, because our businesses happen in the context of His Kingdom, which is already *established*.

In Biblical terms, when God *establishes* something, it just is so – period.

- It's made (e.g. Gen.9:17; Exo. 6:4).
- It's written (e.g. Lev. 26:46; Psa. 78:5).
- It's done, never to be undone (e.g. Dan. 7:27; Psa. 145:13; John 19:30).
- It will never be changed (e.g. 1 Sam. 15:29; Lam. 3:22-23).

Of course, I'm not saying that businesses can't fail just because the owners are Christians. That's clearly not the case; not what we see in the marketplace. You may well have experienced 'failure' yourselves, as a business owner. I have. But what we call 'failures' can be God's greatest successes (the most obvious and world-changing example being Jesus' own death, then resurrection).

No, what I'm saying is that –

> **When we are intentional about bringing our businesses under the certainty of His Established Kingdom, where He is the LORD, our CEO, then we can confidently leave all outcomes in His hand.**

Thus, whether our businesses apparently fail or succeed, becomes irrelevant. Our role is not the outcome, but the input. What's relevant, therefore, is the intentional relationship we establish with Him, through which we *are being transformed into His image from glory to glory...* (2 Cor. 3:18b, NASB)

How, and in what ways, does God establish us? Here are a few examples relevant to business:-

1. *He will be the stability of your times, a wealth of salvation, wisdom and knowledge; the fear of the Lord is his treasure.* (Isa. 33:6, NASB 1995).
2. *When the whirlwind passes, the wicked is no more, but the righteous has an everlasting foundation.* (Prov. 10:25, NASB 1995).
3. *...that in everything you were enriched in Him, in all speech and all knowledge, even as the testimony concerning Christ was confirmed in you, so that you are not lacking in any gift, awaiting eagerly the revelation of our Lord Jesus Christ, who will also confirm you to the end, blameless in the day of our Lord Jesus Christ.* (1 Cor. 1:5-8, NASB 1995).
4. *Therefore humble yourselves under the mighty hand of God, that He may exalt you at the proper time, casting all your anxiety on Him, because He cares for you. Be of sober spirit, be on the alert. Your adversary, the devil, prowls around like a roaring lion, seeking someone to devour. But resist him, firm in your faith, knowing that the same experiences of suffering are being accomplished by your brethren who are in the world. After you have suffered for a little while, the God of all grace, who called you to His eternal glory in Christ, will Himself perfect, confirm, strengthen* and *establish you. To Him be dominion forever and ever. Amen.* (1 Pet. 5:6-11, NASB 1995).

God's involvement is thus always discernible in a business which is started – or which now operates – under His 'new management'. It becomes an expression of His Established Kingdom.

Gill's Story:

Looking back, it's apparent that I had a natural inclination to business even as a kid. At a very young age, I used to make and sell jam sandwiches to friends! At age 11, I needed some money, so I volunteered to wash teachers' cars at lunchtime: it was a success; I even roped friends in.

As I went through school, I took classroom lessons in business, to learn more. Even though I loved it, I wasn't made welcome by the teacher (a woman, interestingly), who favoured the boys, and made it clear that I shouldn't be in the class. In the end I felt sufficiently discouraged that I decided to lay down any hopes of ever starting a business of my own.

Fast forward a lot of years. I'd been married and divorced, and now had a son. About this time, a friend prayed for me, and I had an encounter that changed my life. I was caught up in the Spirit and shown an ancient table. I knew that God the Father was on the other side of this table. Without warning, He asked me, "Gilly, why are you so serious?" — I answered, "Well, apparently I'm in heaven" — and He says, "Apparently". All of a sudden, I was giggling. I found God to be funny! He had a sense of humour, and I loved it.

A curtain drew back, and in front of me was a sea of little brown faces — young children. Father said to me: "Go to them, feed them, clothe them, and tell them that I love them."

"What — now?" I asked. "No", He replied. "I'll tell you when."

I married a second time. Again, sadly, this was an unhappy marriage too, both for me and my son. It ended within a decade but left me emotionally scarred, feeling unworthy, unloved and unvalued.

Shortly after the end of my marriage, a friend phoned me out of the blue and asked, "Gill, there's a child in a hospital overseas — it's dying and needs feeding. I have no money to do anything about it. Will you feed it?" I didn't even ask God whether I should or not — I simply told Him I was going to do it. I mean, what kind of God would He be, if He's not One who saves the vulnerable? It was a no-brainer. What I did ask Him, though, was to help me make it happen. I started paying out of my own savings because I didn't have a job (my son needed near-full-time care at home).

Not long after, she rang again. There were six more.

A while later, there were 100. I took them all on. I'd sold my house by this time to fund the need. Even so, the financial commitment wasn't sustainable. So, I initially started a charity, hoping — wrongly, as it turned out — that the public would help via donations, instead of me just using up all my savings.

Then I had a dream that I was going to sell tea in paper packaging. It would be eco-sustainable as well as making money. I woke up and thought, "OK then, I'd better do just that!"

Then it hit me like a thunderbolt: I suddenly realised that I was anointed for business! I rang my pastor and told her. Her response was very endorsing: "I know", she said. "I didn't", I replied.

But I went to God in prayer. I'd never run a business as an adult, and my self-belief was at an all-time low, although God had always spoken clearly to me about personal issues, so I knew I was safe in His hands. He led me to a specific Bible verse:

> **But remember the Lord your God, for it is He who gives you the ability to produce wealth, and so confirms His covenant, which He swore to your ancestors, as it is today.** (Deut. 8:18 NIV).

So, I formed a limited company and started up the business I'd seen in my dream — only to realise that I was now doing the thing I was born to do!

But don't think it hasn't cost me. I assumed that, because God called me to do it, it would be easy. What I've learned is that He doesn't care about entrepreneurs 'arriving'. He doesn't even really care about our businesses working. His plan is about growing me and about testing me. So I follow, with integrity, the road He's set out in front of me.

Gill Bredl
Charity Tea Limited
https://charitytea.co.nz
(New Zealand)

Time-out, for Reflection:

- Recognising now that your business operates in the context of a Kingdom that's Already Established, how does this change your confidence to move forward, in faith?
- How, and when, will you put aside regular time to apply His strategy and seek His plans, before taking action?

CHAPTER 6
THE IDENTITY-REFLECTING BUSINESS

> *When He had been baptized, Jesus came up immediately from the water; and behold, the heavens were opened to Him, and He saw the Spirit of God descending like a dove and alighting upon Him. And suddenly a voice came from heaven, saying, "This is My beloved Son, in whom I am well pleased."*
> (Matt. 3:16-17, NKJV).

It's our Father who gives us our identity – nothing and no one else.

Jesus had known from a young age that He was the Son of the Father, even though no one else understood it yet – including his parents. You'll remember the story about them taking Him to Jerusalem, aged 12, for the Passover festival. Three days into their journey home, they realised He wasn't with their caravan of travellers, so they returned and found Him...

> *...sitting in the midst of the teachers, both listening to them and asking them questions. And all who heard Him were astonished at His*

> *understanding and answers. So when they saw Him, they were amazed; and His mother said to Him, "Son, why have You done this to us? Look, Your father and I have sought You anxiously." And He said to them, "Why did you seek Me? Did you not know that I must be about My Father's business?" But they did not understand the statement which He spoke to them.* (Luke 2:46b-50, NKJV).

Later, when aged approximately 30, Father nevertheless *announces*, unequivocally, who Jesus is, declaring publicly, 'I'm pleased with Him'. Bear in mind that Jesus hadn't yet done a thing: not performed a miracle, nor told a parable. Not taught crowds, nor challenged the religious leaders of His day. Not yet been to the cross, nor defeated satan – yet Father says, 'I'm pleased with You, Son.'

That's a powerful endorsement. It throws into stark contrast God's wish for us to know that we are who we are *because of Him*, as opposed to our tendency to value ourselves because of the things we do – our achievements.

> It's the cross and resurrection – the pre-established atonement won for us by Jesus – that tells us who we are. Period.

Business implications and application

There are two I want to explore with you.

First:
We, too, need to hear and receive our identity from God, then operate out of it; not look for our business or work to

give us our identity. Asking our business to communicate our worth to us is a destructive road. It results in business activities taking priority over God, self, wife, husband, family, friends, health and hobbies. It becomes possessive of our time and energy. It places some*thing* on the throne of our lives, instead of the Some*One,* who alone is worthy.

> *"For what will it profit a man if he gains the whole world, and loses his own soul?"* (Mark 8:36, NKJV).

> Thus, whilst a business will never give us an honest identity, Kingdom-based businesses can, and should, *reflect* who we are and give us an outlet to *express* our identity.

They're a vehicle through which we convey to the world our confidence in Jesus, and the value He places on us.

As we begin to grasp just who we are 'in Christ, in business', our businesses also allow others to receive that same awareness of Him and of themselves.

Second:
Whatever you do, or don't do, in business – whether you win or lose; make money or not; build a huge conglomerate or enjoy a one-person business; enjoy prestige or prefer to stay in the background; attract public acclaim or are considered a relative nobody – not one of these things affects who we *are* in God.

The only thing that matters is how God sees us: "You are my beloved . . ."

But to benefit from it, we must be willing to accept it. There's no clearer message than this: that we are both friends and sons/daughters of God.[16]

> *"No longer do I call you servants, for a servant does not know what his master is doing; but I have called you friends, for all things that I heard from My Father I have made known to you."* (John 15:15, NKJV).

> *"And it shall come to pass in the place where it was said to them, 'You are not My people,' there they shall be called 'sons of the living God'."* (Rom. 9:26, NKJV – quoting Hosea 1:10).

Just let that soak in for a moment. You are both the confidante, and the offspring, of the One who made the universe and everything in it.

That's a very powerful identity to be given. Receive it!

It calms our fretfulness, slows our fraught-ness, and allows us time to appreciate the beauty of our journey with Him . . . because it's no longer all up to us.

---

[16] I intend no offense by choosing the NKJV for the bulk of my quotes. It has no gender-inclusive edition. I selected it because of its general accuracy to the oldest, original texts. The ancient world was patriarchal, therefore wrote with male pronouns only. But ladies, I want you to be included. For we know that, in Christ, **There is neither Jew nor Greek . . . slave nor free . . .male nor female; for you are all one in Christ Jesus** (Gal. 3:28, NKJV). I honour you.

(To add some humour, if you can accept it - If any reader considers themselves excluded by the NKJV's language, spare a thought for us guys who, along with women, must accept that we're described as the Bride of Christ.)

Entrepreneur's Insights (Myself)

The case of mistaken identity is a deeply personal journey for me.

After a very happy home life as a child, I entered a marriage with a wife who seemed full of life and vivacity. She smiled often, was a high achiever in the medical field, and gave every impression of being a very positive person. But under the surface, her life swam with doubts and self-criticism, at self-damaging levels. Unfortunately, toxicity inside can't help but leak outside, and our marriage became one in which whatever I did or didn't do was never enough.

Inside myself, criticisms compounded, along with a sense of failure. And these built readily on a foundation of severe bullying at school, when I was variously kidnapped, kicked, beaten, and mocked, sometimes by groups of 40 at a time.

Looking for self-worth, I created my own antidote. I became a workaholic. Work was the one sphere in which I felt valued by others, which was affirming. Then, a poor choice of business partners in my first business led me into dishonest actions. This added to our marriage difficulties, resulting in an erosion of trust and an automatic doubt in anything I said at home. Both factors undermined my own self-respect even further. My integrity (a value I'd always prided) was shredded – all because I'd allowed others to incite me to act outside my own values.

My marriage eventually ended, dealing my self-worth another blow. Yet over the following 12 years,

God restored and rebuilt me, giving me a second chance at a – very happy – marriage. He also drove me back into the Scriptures, replacing my tattered self-image with a true understanding of who I am in Him: ransomed, healed, restored, complete and forgiven.

Since then, I've become unexpectedly successful and respected in my chosen field. I no longer look to my work to tell me who I am: I allow only Jesus to do that now.

There are many voices in the world, ready to fill your ears with all sorts of half-truths or untruths. But there's only One Voice who will be absolutely honest with you – even when you find it hard to hear Him because you value yourself so poorly. Jesus alone is the Truth (see John 14:6). Accept what He says about you. He's reliable. It'll change both you and your business, if you do.

Richard's Story:

I had a terrible childhood. I'm the oldest of three boys. My father used to beat my mother just about every day, and me as well, even as a three, four and five year old kid. I could never do anything, ever, that made him proud of me.

In my family, not even my mum (who was the biggest person in my life at that time), said "I love you". I never got approval.

The Identify-Reflecting Business

God has always whispered in my ear, although I didn't realise it then. I therefore tried to conquer business to get that kind of approval. It happened this way.

I owned a chain of fast-food restaurants. It's an industry in which you can't pay high wages to staff – the model doesn't work if you do. Of course, as owner, I knew what each employee was paid.

Since no one had ever shown me approval, I made a deliberate effort to let my staff know that they were valuable to me. I made it a point of getting to know them personally. I talked to them about their homes, their spouses, and their children. I memorised the names of their family members so I could ask them: "How's ......? You told me last month that ...... was happening in their lives. How are things going for them now?"

They were stunned and began to thrive and grow as people. No one had ever cared for them before. They were among the 'forgotten' in our society – the ones others only saw when they were being 'useful'. To most people, they had one function only: "to serve me". Customers certainly didn't see them as individuals, valuable to others and God.

Several times at Christmas, I overheard them talk with one another, saying that they didn't know how they were going to buy presents for their children. So, without them knowing anything about it, I'd go out and buy gifts for every member of their family. I wrapped them, then drove around the town whilst they were at work (I knew their shifts, of course), putting the gifts on their doorsteps. I never told them it was me who did it.

They would come back on their next shift, and excitedly tell me what had happened. I never let on that I knew already. It was such a joy to see the surprise on their faces.

It was as I cared for others – as I realised how important it is to every person to be valued – that I began to realise how much God loved me!

He didn't want me just to believe in Him – He wants me to know Him, as He is. And from that secure awareness of belonging, to share Him with others.

And that's how my sense of identity grew.

Richard
Company owner
(United States)

Time-out, for Reflection:

- To what degree have you been looking to your business, or your 'work persona' – to give you a sense of self-worth, dignity, value, or self-respect?
- Is that one reason you may be struggling to give your business into His control, as your CEO?
- Are you willing to give up your clamouring for self-esteem; to lay it all at the foot of His Cross; to repent and ask God's forgiveness, surrendering to Jesus's leadership of your business?

CHAPTER 7
THE OUTRAGEOUS BUSINESS

> *Now there was a large herd of pigs feeding nearby on the mountain. And the demons begged Him, saying, "Send us into the pigs so that we may enter them." Jesus gave them permission. And coming out, the unclean spirits entered the pigs; and the herd rushed down the steep bank into the sea, about two thousand of them; and they were drowned in the sea. Their herdsmen ran away and reported it in the city and in the countryside. And the people came to see what it was that had happened.*
>
> (Mark 5:11-14, NASB).

You may recognise this as part of Mark's account of Jesus delivering a man possessed of a legion of demons. Three aspects of this event are outrageous.

1. In the process of delivering 'Legion', Jesus appears to have destroyed the economy of an entire region. 2,000 pigs died that day. It was shocking.

2. The location of the city to which the herders "ran away" and reported the loss of the herd is debated[17], but even at five miles/eight kilometres away that's approximately a six-hour round trip after gathering the townsfolk to a meeting. So, Jesus appears to have made this a full day trip, just for the sake of saving a single Gentile. Incomprehensible to His Jewish followers!
3. Jesus was unconcerned and unashamed that His activities that day rendered Him ritually unclean, many times over. He visited tombs (see Num. 19:16); He came into proximity with pigs (see Lev. 11:7); and He interacted with demons/unclean spirits (see Zech. 13:2 and Matt. 10:1).

It's clear that Jesus' only concern was for a man who mattered so immeasurably to His Father, that He crossed a lake to rescue him. Such unfathomable love illustrates the unsearchable passion God expresses to people – a characteristic of His we do well to note in all our own business dealings.

There are many other examples, also, of Jesus scandalising social norms. Here are just a few:-

- He called respected officials 'tombs' (Matt. 23:27) and 'snakes' (Matt. 3:7; 12:34);
- He declared adults can't enter God's Kingdom without becoming neo-nates again (John 3:3-4);

---

[17] For a layman's, but nevertheless helpful, unpacking of the possible sites where this event took place, see
https://biblicalhistoricalcontext.com/gospels/gerasa-gadara-gergesa-from-where-did-the-pigs-stampede/

- He deliberately offended crowds by using language suggesting that they needed to cannibalise Him (John 6:53) – No wonder many of them left as a result (see v. 66 of the same chapter);
- He added turncoats to his central group of followers (Matt. 9:9; Luke 6:16);
- He moved beyond the Mosaic legal requirement to stone an adulterous woman, forgiving her when everyone else condemned her (John 8:1-11);
- He equated Himself with God, claiming His right to forgive sins (Mark 2:5);
- He accepted worship (Matt. 2:11; Matt. 28:9; John 20:28);
- He denounced, in no uncertain terms, corrupt Temple practices (John 2:15; Mark 11:15-17);
- He gave credibility, honour, and salvation to a thief (Luke 23:39-43).

Nature

In addition to Jesus' example, there's a privilege we see every day – although we often miss or ignore it. God expresses an outrageous extravagance, in nature. His artwork is wild, unrestrained, and lavish even though it sometimes comes and goes in mere seconds, never to be repeated.

Think of a cloud formation rolling through, then evaporating; or a sunset that lasts just moments, exclusive to that day; or a snowflake that falls, alights, and melts, gone forever – the loss of its unique structure of no consequence to God. He's apparently unbothered by such brevity, such one-offs. There are plenty more where they came from, in His creative heart.

God places no lasting store on 'things' in our lives – not even His own creativity and beauty. All of earth and heaven will be rolled up one day (see Rev. 6:14), to be replaced by a better version (see Rev. ch. 21). All matter is ultimately dispensable to Him — for He has but to speak one word, and more will appear!

> *The heavens declare the glory of God; the skies proclaim the work of his hands. Day after day they pour forth speech; night after night they reveal knowledge. They have no speech, they use no words; no sound is heard from them. Yet their voice goes out into all the earth, their words to the ends of the world. In the heavens God has pitched a tent for the sun. It is like a bridegroom coming out of his chamber, like a champion rejoicing to run his course. It rises at one end of the heavens and makes its circuit to the other; nothing is deprived of its warmth.* (Psa. 19:1-6, NIV).

Quite amazing. God appears to paint such extraordinary cosmic canvasses in a bid to inspire us to deep awe at His limitlessness. His heart explodes with imagination; a creativity He also yearns to lavish on *people* — on us, our businesses, and those served and embraced through them.

For we humans are the crown of His creation. He will give us — and remove from us — whatever He deems necessary (see Job 1:21) to express the depths of His love to us and to inspire faith in us, as unique individuals. His is an outrageous dedication — especially since we do not deserve it.

Business implications and application

To Jesus, there are two things that matter above all else: His Father, and people. More than products, services, profits, growth, adherence to social requirements, and every other common measure of commercial success. In fact, *anything* that gets in the way either of God Himself being glorified, or of people being valued as individuals, He will undermine and rebuke (see Luke 19:45-46; John 14:13; Luke 4:18-19). Therefore, quite simply, we need to be the same.

Have you heard businesses claim: "Our company's a family; our people are our most important assets"? If so, have you seen the duplicity and deception in those statements?

1) *A family and a business are two totally different things.*

Family Members	Company Employees
Are wanted because of love.	Are wanted to fulfil commercial goals.
Places of nurture.	Places of productivity.
Are embraced after making mistakes.	Are disciplined for making mistakes.
Belong permanently, by right – either born-in, or adopted.	Engaged temporarily, for specific tasks. Never belong as of right.
When "useless" (through illness or age) are still valued and actively cared for.	When "useless" are disposable and either encouraged to leave, or restructured out.
Those with whom we share life's joys and pleasures.	Those expected to generate profits and enhance cash balances for us.
Value is in the person themselves.	Value is in what they can do for the company.

2) *The very suggestion that people are "assets" is dehumanising.*

"Asset" is an objective word, an investment term, denoting possessions acquired, whose value lies in their ability to increase financial wealth.[18]

By contrast, Jesus treated people quite the opposite. Everyone He met who'd been degraded, marginalised or dehumanised, *He elevated with dignity*:-

- Gentiles (e.g. Matt. 15:21-28);
- Lepers (e.g. Luke 17:11-19);
- Ritually 'unclean' people (e.g. Luke 8:43-48);
- Samaritans (e.g. John 4:7-26);
- Women (e.g. Luke 7:36-50);
- Tax collectors (e.g. Luke 19:1-10);
- Children (e.g. Luke 18:15-17).

Do you remember the worship song, "Jesus, be the centre"? When we truly understand this as our deepest *need*, then our businesses will start to express 'Kingdom'. Because –

> **God is willing, if necessary, to destroy businesses, economies – indeed *any* of our 'idols' – in order to gain our attention, and to restore us to an unbroken relationship with Him, through Jesus.**

---

[18] "Human Resources" is, in my opinion, no better. A resource is something inanimate, used to achieve someone else's goal. It does not value the person as a person. At no time did Jesus **ever** treat any individual as though they were a mere 'resource'.

Pete and Alanna's Story

Alanna was introduced to business, both through her parents' activities and by taking a commerce degree at college. Pete had made his career in wine and was a manager at his parent's boutique winery in North Canterbury, New Zealand. Although Pete loved the vineyard, both of us sensed, in our prayers, a need to get ready for change. We couldn't see how working in viticulture would 'fit' in the long-term, as we had a sense that our work would be connected to helping others. We started to assume we'd be called into mission work or something similar, as a result. We'd been praying for a while, "Lord, we'd love to be of use to You," . . . but we never imagined that, when His answer came, it would keep us here in New Zealand, still working in the wine world!

We went on an overseas vacation to visit friends. It changed everything!

It was Christmas Eve in Kolkata, India. The friends we were visiting there ran a business that offers alternative employment opportunities to women who'd been in prostitution. Deciding to visit one of the women we'd met, we took a shortcut through an alleyway. Standing to one side were a group of teenage girls who looked distinctly different. Asking why, we were told they'd been trafficked from Nepal and sold into prostitution. In that moment, the penny dropped: We had just passed modern-day slaves.

The injustice of it hit us hard. No one should be sold for someone else's profit. That was never in Jesus' repertoire of 'people treatment'. Most think we left slavery behind last century, but that couldn't be further from the truth. There are more people in slavery today than ever before. Twenty-one million is the conservative estimate – the Global Slavery Index suggests 40.3 million. Either way – 21.0 or 40.3 million – it's far too many.

It was an issue that demanded our attention; but knowing how to respond was the difficult part. Pete's career (as vineyard manager) and slavery didn't seem like a natural fit!

That was, until we had a 'what if' moment. Lots of people drink wine...so, what if we started a company and created a wine where 100% of the profits go towards helping to end slavery? It seemed crazy, but crucial. So we started.

We decided to call the wine (and our company) '27seconds' after a UNICEF statistic. They estimate 1.2 million children are sold into slavery every year. When you average that out, it works out as one every 27 seconds.

Our goal is simple: make good wine, sell lots of it commercially, then give our profits to organisations working to end slavery.

It's outrageous in its audacity, really, because we can't, and won't, solve modern-day slavery; but we and our customers can – and do – play a real part in helping.

Pete and Alanna Chapman
Business owners, 27 Seconds Limited
www.27seconds.co.nz
(New Zealand)

Time-out, for Reflection:

- How has God shown Himself to be outrageous in your business?
- How well do you embrace extravagant creativity in your business? Do you value it, or downplay it?
- In what ways do you need to start or continue expressing the audacious humanity of Jesus?
- Are you ready and willing to alter anything He's showing you, as you've reflected?

CHAPTER 8
THE ATTRACTIVE BUSINESS

He has no form or comeliness; and when we see Him, there is no beauty that we should desire Him. He is despised and rejected by men, a Man of sorrows and acquainted with grief. And we hid, as it were, our faces from Him; He was despised, and we did not esteem Him.

(Isa. 53:2b-3, NKJV).

So it was, when Jesus returned, that the multitude welcomed Him, for they were all waiting for Him.

(Luke 8:40, NKJV).

Hollywood loves to portray Jesus as a stunningly handsome, good-looking man, with blemish-less skin, perfect teeth, colour-enhanced eyes, with flowing locks of perfectly shampooed and combed long hair. Yet the above passage from Isaiah suggests there was nothing remarkable about the way He looked. For all we know, Jesus might have been short and very plain. He probably had sun-dried skin if He'd worked as a carpenter with Joseph; and He certainly wouldn't have used Western soaps or after-shave to smell good.

Yet, people flocked to Him!

True, He was a miracle-worker; and we know some came for no better reason than to get a free meal (see John 6:26). But the above verse from Luke states that all the people were "waiting for Him".

His personality was clearly attractive.

Even little children were magnetised by Him. Something about Him held their interest and attention. They allowed Him to pick them up and hug them.

> *And He took them up in His arms, laid His hands on them, and blessed them.* (Mark 10:16, NKJV).

Other socially powerless people couldn't resist Him either. Once, a prostitute gate-crashed a private dinner party to ensure Jesus wouldn't leave before she'd had the opportunity to express her shame and need of forgiveness, in extraordinary vulnerability:

> *And behold, a woman in the city who was a 'sinner', when she knew that Jesus sat at the table in the Pharisee's house, brought an alabaster flask of fragrant oil, and stood at His feet behind Him weeping; and she began to wash His feet with her tears, and wiped them with the hair of her head; and she kissed His feet and anointed them with the fragrant oil.* (Luke 7:37-38, NKJV).

What made Him so attractive?

Business implications and application

It's an important question if our businesses are to express such attractiveness – His attractiveness. We won't achieve it by being risqué or clever, by having specials, by developing new products or services or through any other business techniques. Marketing – even though it has value – can't achieve human charisma either.

No, what makes businesses attractive is the deliberate, consistent expression of Jesus' own character into the world *through us*.

We can't do that by trying. We can't visualise it into being[19], will it into existence, nor pretend[20]. Nor can we take classes in being 'Jesus-like', as though His character is up for grabs via a 2-hour seminar. All of these are attempts to work *for* Him rather than *with* Him.

There's only one way to become as attractive as Jesus, and that's to let Him do so, in us.

When we allow Him to mould our characters; as we deny ourselves, take up our Cross and follow Him (see Matt. 16:24), that's when His character is expressed in and through us. In other words, it's His sovereign work, not as a result of any effort of our own.

---

[19] Visualisation is a current trend in the teaching of life and business coaches. It's the self-absorbed counterfeit for the visions and dreams that God Himself gives (e.g. see Job 33:14-15; Joel 2:28-29).

[20] 'Fake it till you make it' – whilst a popular sales teaching – is also a self-absorbed counterfeit. Lying to get the outcomes that serve us is in direct opposition to Jesus' teaching about honesty and integrity. However, there is a way for us to succeed that God approves – see Prov. 3:3-6 and Prov. 16:3, for example.

> Although salvation is a free gift, discipleship costs us everything. Running a business as a faithful expression of His Kingdom, is a discipleship activity.

And it takes time.

But imagine: just how attractive *could* a company be, to customers, suppliers, staff, and third parties, if we invited Holy Spirit to develop His fruit in us and all our business dealings?

> *But the fruit of the Spirit is love, joy, peace, longsuffering, kindness, goodness, faithfulness, gentleness, self-control. Against such there is no law.* (Gal. 5:22-23, NKJV).

What if we wholeheartedly surrendered our egos to Him, and embraced obedience, just as Jesus did?

> *Let this mind be in you which was also in Christ Jesus . . . He humbled Himself and became obedient to the point of death, even the death of the cross. Therefore God also has highly exalted Him...* (Phil. 2:5,8b-9a, NKJV).

Jesus' attractiveness was formed through His reliance on the relationship He enjoyed with His Father. He —

- Maintained transparency (*I and the Father are one* — John 10:30, NIV);
- Enjoyed His company (*At daybreak, Jesus went out to a solitary place* — Luke 4:42a, NIV);
- Listened to Him (*I am telling you what I have seen in the Father's presence* — John 8:38a, NIV);

- Acted only out of that relationship, as He listened to Holy Spirit leading Him to do so (e.g. the chance meeting of a funeral procession at Nain, where He raised from death, the son of a widow – see Luke 7:11-17).

Do we dare to take Jesus at His word, and follow His example, trusting Him for the outcome? Or are you perhaps tempted to feel discouraged by the apparent impossibility of developing such a relationship, and experiencing such attractiveness? If so, please don't, because –

1) Jesus advised us – through a prayer He prayed Himself, on our behalf – that we are eligible to enjoy *exactly the same relationship that He had with Father*:-

    ...that they all may be one, as You, Father, are in Me, and I in You; that they also may be one in Us, that the world may believe that You sent Me (John 17:21, NKJV);

– and furthermore –

2) He continues to intercede for, and defend, us –

    Who is he who condemns? It is Christ who died, and furthermore is also risen, who is even at the right hand of God, who also makes intercession for us. (Rom. 8:34, NKJV).

    If God is for us, who can be against us. (Rom. 8:31b, NKJV).

It is through the work of Christ in us that we can change — until we, too, begin to reflect His incredibly attractive nature, personality and character to those around us, in business.

Andrew's Story

I was working overseas, in China. In late June of 1999, a young secretary who worked for me, was kidnapped.

After some pretty frightening events, and through her own sharp wits, she managed to escape, noting the registration number of the car used to snatch her. Her father, who was in the provincial government, took her to the police station to report the incident.

But when the police checked, they found it was an army number plate, and they refused to get involved or take any action, despite her father's important role — because the army was known to be 'a law unto itself', not to be trifled with.

Next day, phone calls began to the young lady. The kidnappers had stolen her bag, so they had her identification. Five or six times that Monday, her office phone rang, and the voice on the other end said, "Lady, we know where you work, we know where you live. We're going to come and kill you."

Day after day the threats continued throughout the week. I was part of a fellowship which held a prayer meeting on the last Friday of every month; so on the Friday afternoon, I said to her, "Tonight my friends and I are going to pray that God will deliver you".

She said, "Thank you, but no one can succeed against the Chinese army".

A group of us prayed that evening that God would intervene; but when I got to work on the Monday, she hadn't waited for supernatural help. She told me her father was arranging to get her a job far away in the north of the country, so she would be out of the kidnappers' reach.

I knew that the company needed to support her – and we could only do so by depending on the power of God. I replied, "This is ridiculous! Tomorrow I'll go to the police myself". She replied, "No one can do anything against the army in our country: it's too powerful." Yet I was confident of God, and answered, "God is more powerful than the army".

However, as I went home that day, I began to feel nervous; had I been a bit rash? What if I went to the police and nothing happened? After all, if her father and his government connections couldn't help, what could I do? I'd made claims to her which, unless God intervened, wouldn't happen – for I have no control over the Almighty! The results were out of my hands; the only thing I could control was my prayer, and my actions.

I started to pray earnestly about it, and asked God to show me clearly whether I'd been presumptuous. Also, should I, or shouldn't I get involved? As an 'interfering foreigner', was I just stirring up a hornet's nest that could make things worse for her?

Yet we'd prayed on the Friday night for her deliverance — something I know is in line with God's will, being part of Jesus' disclosed manifesto (Luke 4:18-19).

As I was going to bed, I remembered that I had not turned over the next page of a desk calendar I had, so I did so. On it was 2 Chronicles 20:15-17. As I read it, it was as if the words were flames of fire leaping off the page at me:

> **"This is what the Lord says to you: 'Do not be discouraged because of this vast army. For the battle is not yours, but God's. Tomorrow march down against them...you will not have to fight this battle...stand firm and see the deliverance of the Lord. Go out and face them tomorrow, and the Lord will be with you'."**

If ever God had spoken directly to me in the very circumstances I was facing, this was it! China's army is the largest military force in the world, over two-and-a-quarter million strong — a vast army indeed!

So, the next morning I went with the young lady, to the police station, and spoke to the desk sergeant. I said, "This young lady and her father came here 10 days ago to report that she'd been kidnapped; could you tell me what progress has been made?"

"Who are you?" the desk sergeant asked. I gave him the name of my company, and said, "I am the General Manager where this lady works".

"As far as I am aware, the case is closed", he said. "Your employee has escaped; she is unharmed; and since the car involved is an army vehicle, there is really nothing we can do."

That could have been the end of the conversation but for some reason he continued: "However, as you have taken the trouble to come in, sir, I will report upstairs to the Chief of Police and let him know you were enquiring. Please, go back to work, and we will call you later."

I thought, "Wow! I didn't have to fight any battle, just as God promised. So, what does He have planned? What is He going to do?"

The response from the young lady herself, and other Chinese colleagues was very negative. They said, "The police are just fobbing you off politely because you are a foreigner. You will hear nothing more. They can do nothing against the army!"

But at three o'clock that afternoon, a call was put through to my office. On the other end was the Chief of Police. He said "Sir, we have identified the car as belonging to a construction company, part-owned by the military. We have contacted the appropriate senior officials, and they have traced the driver as a man named Chen. They will deal with this matter internally. They have asked me to apologise to you, and promise that these criminals will never bother the young lady, or your company again". And they never did!

The young lady's parents expressed their gratitude to me, adding, "Perhaps foreigners have some use after all!"

But the young lady in question realised that this had been God acting for her good, and a short while later started attending a Chinese church and came to faith in Jesus. He had shown Himself powerful and attractive; and drew her to Himself.

Andrew Kelly
Former General Manager in China
(United Kingdom)

Time-out, for Reflection:

- Have you thought before of Jesus being able to express His attractiveness through your business? If not, how does that now change both –
    - The possibilities in your personal relationship with Him? – and
    - The possible opportunities for your business?
- What might you need to surrender to Jesus, either in your personal or business life?
- In what areas of your life or business have you resisted Him, or His love and grace?
    - Why?
    - What is He asking you to do about it?
- Take time to respond to Him, before reading further.

CHAPTER 9
THE UPSIDE-DOWN BUSINESS

> *And seeing the multitudes, He went up on a mountain, and when He was seated His disciples came to Him. Then He opened His mouth and taught them, saying: "Blessed are . . . "*
> (Matt. 5:1-3a, NKJV).

Jesus' teaching, and His life, was unnervingly alternative. Everything He did upset the status quo. The detail of the Jewish Law was intended to position people into relationship with God; yet Jesus extended it way beyond anything they'd ever conceived. In doing so, He challenged society to its very core.

I believe God wants to challenge us to the core, also, as business owners. True, we no longer live under Moses' Law, but have we created our own counterfeit code for living and business? Will we let Him prod us, question us, provoke us, to find out where we've tried to turn His gospel right-way-up again, suiting our needs, instead of His?

> *Search me, O God, and know my heart; try me,... see if there is any wicked way in me, and lead me in the way everlasting.* (Psa. 139:23-24, NKJV).

The first thing I notice about the Sermon on the Mount, is that, when Jesus saw 'the multitude', He deliberately climbed a mountain – apparently to put off those reluctant to put in the effort of coming too. Who was genuinely interested to know the truth of the gospel of the Kingdom of God; and who was just a casual observer or 'wonder-hunter', preferring their current inadequate understanding?

Business implications and application

Can our businesses be 100% grounded on Jesus' alternative example?

If we take Him seriously, we dare not merely dabble in our Christian faith. To do so is to risk our mouths saying one thing, whilst our hearts live another. Our duplicity will prevent others from seeing their attractive Saviour, through our businesses.

Taking Him seriously means adopting all His Upside-Down conditions, including those that 'just don't make sense' in a corporate world that's driven by different standards.

- His requirement that we stop being timid about Him and start standing up and being counted:
  "You are the light of the world. A town built on a hill cannot be hidden. Neither do people light a lamp and put it under a bowl. Instead they put it on its stand, and it gives light to everyone in the house." (Matt. 5:14-15, NKJV);

- His assertion that anger is the same as murder, breaching one of the 10 commandments:
  "You have heard that it was said to the people long ago, 'You shall not murder, and anyone

who murders will be subject to judgment.' But I tell you that anyone who is angry with a brother or sister will be subject to judgment." (Matt. 5:21-22a, NKJV);

- Or that lust is no different to adultery, breaking a second of the 10 commandments:
  "You have heard that it was said, 'You shall not commit adultery.' But I tell you that anyone who looks at a woman lustfully has already committed adultery with her in his heart." (Matt. 5:27-28, NIV);

- What about this non-negotiable condition, that His followers must love, bless and do good to our enemies?
  "...love your enemies, bless those who curse you, do good to those who hate you, and pray for those who spitefully use you and persecute you." (Matt. 5:44, NKJV);

- Or another non-negotiable: that only servants are allowed to be leaders in His Kingdom's corporations:
  "...whoever desires to become great among you shall be your servant." (Mark 10:43b, NKJV);

- In Kingdom businesses, He says, we owners may not consider our needs before those of others:
  "He who loves his life will lose it, and he who hates his life in this world will keep it for eternal life." (John 12:25, NASB);

- And that we must embrace the truth that grace and weakness serve the world, not strength:
  "My grace is sufficient for you, for My strength is made perfect in weakness." (2 Cor. 12:9a, NKJV);

- And perhaps the most Upside-Down of all:
  "So the last will be first, and the first last. For many are called, but few chosen." (Matt. 20:16, NKJV).

Truly, Kingdom business owners have some challenges.

In contrast, Western society and the commercial marketplace both place expectations on us, for self-promotion, self-aggrandisement, acquisition of the material trappings of success, applause of adversarial relationships, and a win-at-all-costs attitude. They judge the clothes we all dress in, what we drive, where we live, and with whom we socialise. Measurable outcomes take precedence over human worth, short-term gains govern their KPIs, and the supremacy of the dollar is a silent driver in all decisions and attitudes. Companies work to please stakeholders rather than God, and their cultures and ways of communicating lack transparency – and more.

> **It's far too easy to absorb the values of our society, and *never even to be aware that we have*.**

How, then, are we to respond? What's the answer?

Before we throw ourselves into a crusade on corrective actions, let's make our first port of call the examination of our own hearts. With surrender, Jesus' power is accessible to us, to embrace the responsibility and thrill of living the Upside-Down life God calls us into, in business.

> *"...seek first the kingdom of God and His righteousness, and all these things shall be added to you."* (Matt. 6:33, NKJV).

"All these things" refers to verses 25-32 before, in which He's challenged His hearers not to worry about their lives, food- and drink-supplies, clothes, the seasons; and work expectations.

Jesus' express command is "do not worry", because —

> *"...your Father knows the things you have need of before you ask Him."* (Matt. 6:8b, NKJV).

A word about money in particular

Money is inert, inanimate, and therefore without moral value. Neither making it nor owning it is either good or bad. Jesus began His life, as a baby, with a chest of gold given Him by eastern wise-men (Matt. 2:11); and during at least part of His ministry, He wore a robe made with no seams — indicative of a costly garment (John 19:23). He wasn't fazed by His wealth, nor did He hang onto it, preferring the freedom of the open road to the ownership of houses and other possessions.

However, money can, and does, become a snare when we want it and prioritise it, especially for self-centred purposes. In that setting, it dominates, trapping us in a powerful mindset of idolatry, irrespective of whether we own a lot of it or only a little.

The Upside-Down Kingdom requires that we must let it go, emotionally. Only then will it no longer control us. Interestingly, once that happens, we often find ourselves making and managing more of it — possibly because God now trusts us to manage it rightly, for Him.

Paul was a tent-maker, probably to the merchant-caravan

industry. He offers business owners valuable insight into what our attitudes to money and wealth need to be, in order for God to trust us with large helpings of His Kingdom's resources:

> *...for I have learned to be content in whatever circumstances I am. I know how to get along with little, and I also know how to live in prosperity; in any and every circumstance I have learned the secret of being filled and going hungry, both of having abundance and suffering need. I can do all things through Him who strengthens me.* (Phil. 4:11b-13, NASB).

Paul's apparent nonchalance to money came not from a disinterest in it, but from an unshakeable assurance that his needs *would* be met – in fact, more than met. I can imagine Paul saying: 'Because I operate exclusively and determinedly out of God's upside-down Kingdom values, where His wishes are infinitely more important than my needs, why would I ever worry about profit? It's God's job to take care of that, whilst my part is to listen, hear and obey.'

> *And my God will supply all your needs according to His riches in glory in Christ Jesus.* (Phil 4:19, NASB).

Although challenging to the core, is this a proposition you're ready and willing to adopt?

My Story

> *In 2016 I left my role as a Managing Director, convinced the time was right to seek a new direction. After six months, I'd put out close to 100 job*

applications and — despite the 'hand-in-glove-fit' my experience offered in some cases, I was invited to only six interviews in total and wasn't offered one of the jobs (not something I'd experienced previously).

Sensing God was doing something different from any previous job-hunt, I went away with three friends, who invited me to a 24-hour retreat. After a brief meeting, we went to our own rooms for the duration. My prayer was, "Father, I'm confused by what's been happening. You know my heart better than I do. Would You please reveal to me what it is I really want!"

About halfway through the retreat, I sensed a reply: "Your next role will be one in which you will live out of your own values every day." I questioned further what that meant, but had to be content with just that, as my answer.

Of course, I did next what we're all prone to do (including Abraham, after his promise of a son!) — I tried to work out how I could fulfil this plan of God's, through my own wisdom and actions! "What roles might give me that?", I wondered. "Perhaps something in the NGO market?" I started throwing out job applications into that sector. Needless to say, not one resulted in anything.

A month or so later, someone I knew spoke to me at the end of a church service: "Have you ever thought of becoming a business consultant? I think you could be good at that."

"Thanks", I answered, ungraciously, "but not a chance! I've been self-employed a number of times, *and don't wish to head back down that route."*

To cut a long story short, a second asked me the same question a few weeks later. Then two others – a husband and wife (both consultants themselves, in international contexts). When I still resisted, a fifth was sent to me . . . and finally a sixth. God wouldn't give up! He kept at me, wearing down my resistance, until I began to acknowledge His hand in it.

Things got even more exciting once I started. God brought me clients again and again, throughout my four years with the Consulting Group.

Our engagements were open-ended, often with only six to eight clients at a time. For some strange reason I still don't fathom, my clients often brought their engagements to an end in 'bunches' of three. When the first three did so, I went to God in prayer: "How do You and I get more clients this time, Lord? What would you like me to do?" His reply: "Don't do anything. I have some referrals coming to you."

Within six weeks, I'd had five referrals, three of whom became clients. It was God's strategy for the moment. I haven't had that many referrals at once, before or since.

A year later, another three ended their engagements, six weeks apart from one another. Once more I asked God in prayer, "What would You like me to do this time, Lord?" He answered, "Wait a month – I've got a different plan this time." One month later, one of my colleagues left the business unexpectedly and I was asked to take on three of his clients. Once again,

without input on my part, God met my need.
"Seek first the kingdom of God and His righteousness, and all these things shall be added to you", *Jesus said.* (Matt. 6:33, NKJV).

Other times, I've found clients through normal commercial means – making contact with unknown businesses, using a telemarketer, etc. He knows the clients we need to work with and is able to bring all parties together – and sometimes, to reinforce His sovereignty, He chooses to do so with no input from us. Ask. Listen. Follow His lead, even when it's counter-intuitive, as in my case: "Stop – don't do a thing!" He works His Upside-Down Kingdom His way, if we'll let Him.

Peter

Time-out, for Reflection:

- Does the need to operate His way, as presented in this chapter, perhaps scare you a little? If so, how will you and Jesus address your fears together?
- Where have you missed out in the past, by trying to retain control, wanting Him to fit into your expectations? What is God asking you to change, surrender, or sacrifice to Him?
- What might be some exciting outcomes from making the changes He's asking of you?
- What new hope rises up in you, as a result?

CHAPTER 10
THE FORGIVING BUSINESS

Then Peter came up and said to Him, "Lord, how many times shall my brother sin against me and I still forgive him? Up to seven times?" Jesus said to him, "I do not say to you up to seven times, but up to seventy-seven times.

For this reason the Kingdom of heaven is like a king who wanted to settle accounts with his slaves.....
(Matt. 18:21-23, NASB).

For if you forgive other people for their offenses, your heavenly Father will also forgive you. But if you do not forgive other people, then your Father will not forgive your offenses.
(Matt. 6:14-15, NASB).

Forgiveness is a Kingdom of God issue; Jesus makes that perfectly clear. It's not optional for those who want to live under the mercy of God's full and rich blessing. Failing or refusing to forgive is the 'unforgiveable sin' – at least until we repent. It's serious.

It can also be difficult. Why? Because there are times when it just seems so unfair for someone to get away with something they've done – whether against us, or others, or repeatedly. But bluntly – that's not our concern.

I used to think that I couldn't forgive, because my emotions kept holding on to the sense of injustice; and I felt that until my emotions got in line, my forgiveness wasn't genuine. Then I was shown a different way of understanding forgiveness.[21] I hope it helps you, as it's helped me, to forgive anyone who's ever wronged me wholeheartedly and generously. It's released me to love again, which is what Jesus asks of us:

> *"But I say to you who hear: Love your enemies, do good to those who hate you, bless those who curse you, and pray for those who spitefully use you."* (Luke 6:27-28, NKJV).

There are four steps to understanding forgiveness:

a) What Forgiveness is *not!*

It's not –
- Letting the other person "off the hook".
- A passive acceptance of what's happened to us.
- Thinking that Jesus wants us to be a doormat and just to "suck it up".
- Pretending that what happened was OK.
- Pretending I don't mind.
- Pretending that I now like them (or believing that God now wants me to like them) despite what they've done.

---

[21] My sincere thanks to my close friend and pastor, Johno Melville, for sharing these understandings with me, and encouraging me to share them with others. You are a true Brother in the faith.

- Saying that what they did is "alright". (If they've done something to hurt us, that's definitely *not* OK!)
- Saying that if they do it again, it's OK.

b) **What Forgiveness *is!***

- Forgiveness is a legal process in God's realm, actioned in the law court of Heaven (see 2 Cor. 5:10), whereby we and God, together, acknowledge the wrongs done to us or someone else, and then choose to give up to Him, the right to redress those wrongs.
- Scripture uses legal language to explain the Heavenly realm. The spiritual legal system was set up by God Himself, just as He set up physical laws in the universe. All created beings are subject to His established order. His Kingdom is ruled over by God. There's a Judge (the Father on His throne); a Prosecuting Counsel (satan the accuser – see Rev. 12:10) and a Defence Counsel (Jesus Himself – our Intercessor and Advocate – see Rom. 8:34 and 1 John 2:1). In the book of Job we see satan coming to accuse Job before the Throne of God – it's a legal setting, in which satan may not act without God's authorisation.

c) **Forgiveness is a legal transaction, not an emotional one. It's most easily understood by first understanding *Unforgiveness:-***

At its core, unforgiveness is two things:-
- A decision made by me/us that the person who has wronged me/us *deserves* to be judged. This is tantamount to saying, "Father, would you mind hopping off the Throne for a moment, because I

know what's best here, and that person deserves harsh judgement and a penalty".

This is actually idolatry, where we unseat God in favour of something or someone else taking His place – ourselves, on this occasion.

- A wish to see them punished and hurting, because of what they did, either to us or someone else. This is taking vengeance; and Scripture says:

"Never take your own revenge, beloved, but leave room for the wrath of God, for it is written: 'Vengeance is Mine, I will repay,' says the Lord." (see Rom. 12:19, NASB).

When these were first explained to me, I was shocked and horrified at the implications of my actions and attitudes. This should be 'salvation 101' . . . yet I'd missed it! The good news is that they give us the keys to allowing us to forgive genuinely and powerfully.

d) *Forgiveness*, therefore, is:-

- A legal declaration, made in Heaven's court before the Father, to give judgement and vengeance back into His hands.
  This is a decision. What a relief to find that our emotions don't drive the truth of whether we can forgive or not. A decision does. Our obedient choice to surrender to God's authority comes first . . . our emotions can catch up later, when they're ready.
- Our only right to access Heaven, and make legal declarations there, is as a result of the atonement of Jesus, Who opened a way for us to be restored into relationship with the Father (see Heb. 10:20).

Business implications and application

Business owners experience the requirement to forgive in business contexts, just as much as that need crops up in every other aspect of our lives. Suppliers, employees, customers, the owners of other businesses – they can wrong us, cheat us, steal from us, damage our reputations, or undermine us in other ways. How we react to that, as owners of Kingdom-based businesses is critical.

Failing to forgive, means God will not forgive us. We fall outside of the boundaries of His Kingdom, and therefore of His protection . . . until we are willing to lay down our own determination to be the jury and judge, and our own demand to have a right to avenge ourselves.

How terrifying to deny our businesses the protection and blessings of God's Kingdom, just so that we may satisfy some emotion or other that 'feels good' by refusing to forgive.

> *It is a fearful thing to fall into the hands of the living God.* (Heb. 10:31, NKJV)[22].

---

[22] Reading this verse in its full context gives sharp clarity to the warning we are being given:

> *For if we sin willfully after we have received the knowledge of the truth, there no longer remains a sacrifice for sins, but a certain fearful expectation of judgment, and fiery indignation which will devour the adversaries. Anyone who has rejected Moses' law dies without mercy on the testimony of two or three witnesses. Of how much worse punishment, do you suppose, will he be thought worthy who has trampled the Son of God underfoot, counted the blood of the covenant by which he was sanctified a common thing, and insulted the Spirit of grace? For we know Him who said, "Vengeance is Mine, I will repay," says the Lord. And again, "The Lord will judge His people." It is a fearful thing to fall into the hands of the living God.* (Heb. 10:26-31, NKJV)

Never forget: the one you want to judge belongs to Another. You have no right to harm them. Your only righteous course of action – taking up your cross and following Him – is to release them to One who judges all humanity righteously.

Joel and Nikki's Story

We met at art college. We were married 10 weeks after our first date and pregnant eight weeks later. That became the blueprint for our lives: we decide, commit and make things happen.

Art college courses don't lead automatically to income generation.

About 18 months after our marriage, we were broke, so made our own Christmas cards that year. Our first child's scribbles were on the front, and our own artwork was on the back. People went nuts over our idea. All the parents at our nursery school wanted us to make cards for them too. Before long we were selling thousands of cards in a number of schools. We realised we'd stumbled onto a business opportunity – and it was profitable.

We called ourselves Vanilla Card Company, created a really attractive brand, and started getting orders left, right and centre via our new website.

With no prior business experience, we got a business advisor. He helped us get some funding, then suggested that we move closer to his printing factory, three hours away, so he could be of more help to us.

We found a great church in the area, which helped us to agree. His company paid for a car, mobile phones, and even found a house for us to live in. He even arranged for American investors to come over, talking to us about getting our cards into the USA.

We went to a number of business expos that year, signing up over 200,000 families with young kids, who all wanted us to make Christmas cards for them that year. Each would buy at least one pack of cards. Aged just 24, we thought we'd made it.

We got back to the factory after one of the expos and his accountant asked us to sign some forms 'about the limited company'. We were naïve. We trusted his explanations and signed the forms, discovering afterwards that we'd been duped. We'd signed ownership of our company over to our advisor. He told us we could now either work for him or leave. We decided to leave – which, of course, meant giving up the house, phones, and car too.

We got the ombudsman and local MP involved. They managed to arrange the wiping of a loan, but could help no further.

Forgiveness is powerfully releasing. It's a gift to yourself, nothing to do with the other person. When you forgive, you release yourself from the judgement and the responsibility you feel towards the other person. We made a purposeful decision to release him, and set our sights forward only. We were young, had loads of energy, and could either put our efforts into resenting the past, or moving forward. We weren't going back.

God honoured that decision. We started again from scratch, with just £500 to our name. We had to apply for tax credits just to buy new printing supplies.

God protected us and met our faith. In the first year, we got new premises, a new printer, then our first staff member, and turned over enough to keep us afloat. Each of the next two years our turnover doubled, which confirmed for us that we were going in the right direction.

We've learned that the guts of forgiveness, is learning to pray for and bless the person who's wronged us. Bless everything they're doing, everything they are, their family, kids, relationships. In that process, you learn that everyone's just another person. We're all as fragile as each other really; all of us emotional wrecks in one way or another! It softens you and allows you to forgive.

The Beatitudes teach that blessing is about acknowledging the faithfulness of God. It's not about the things that we receive; it's about us recognising His faithfulness more and more. Early on in our marriage God said to us, "I can create anything from nothing. Keep giving out, and I will provide all of your needs." He's proven Himself faithful!

Joel and Nikki Buckley
Buckley & Buckley Limited
(United Kingdom)

Time-out, for Reflection:

- The following are some specific action steps for forgiveness I've found helpful. By all means use them if they are helpful for you too:-

  A powerful prayer – a "legal declaration" – submitting to God
  The following prayer aims to embody the understandings of forgiveness set out in this chapter:

  Father, in the Name of Jesus, I forgive [person] for [acknowledge and name the specific wrong they've done]. I now release them from my judgement and renounce all vengeance against them.

- As part of your willing obedience, don't forget to forgive:-
    - Everyone whom you believe contributed to each situation, or allowed it by keeping silent;
    - God Himself, if you've blamed Him for the injustice of the situation or for not getting you out of it sooner;
    - Yourself, if you've spoken words of self-contempt, blame, loathing, or anger over yourself. (Such words are actually acts of 'self-cursing'. Use the Name of Jesus as your authority, to declare that the effects of any such a curse are now broken.)

- This is an act of submission, in which we –
    - Reinstate God as rightful Judge, and
    - Accept wholeheartedly that however He deals with the individuals, including by offering them

the same grace He has shown to us, we will acknowledge it gladly, as righteous.

CHAPTER 11
THE SACRIFICIAL BUSINESS

Then Jesus said to His disciples, "If anyone desires to come after Me, let him deny himself, and take up his cross, and follow Me."
                                    (Matt. 16:24, NKJV).

"...unless a grain of wheat falls into the ground and dies, it remains alone; but if it dies, it produces much grain."
                                    (John 12:24, NKJV).

I made many stupid mistakes when I first went into business as a novice entrepreneur. I poured every hour of every day, and half of my nights at times, into my new business. My family suffered. I became an absentee husband and father for too many years. Sometimes a grumpy one too, wearing 'busy-ness' like a badge of honour, so I could feel important.

I realise now that I asked my family, not myself, to make the sacrifices. I was too busy enjoying the exciting rush, the thrill-of-the-chase, to notice that I wasn't fulfilling Jesus' expectation. But His word is clear. I was the one who needed to deny myself; I was the grain of wheat needing to die.

For a while, I felt alive — incongruously so since the long-term results damaged my health via burnout and depression, then ended my first marriage. For many years I lost the respect and closeness of my three children also. Now, fortunately, they've all been restored, by the grace of God.

Can you relate to my story? I hope not — although I suspect some readers will.

So, let me ask you this: Does all that sound like something God *intends* for His children, when He calls us into business? Surely not!

Even when Jesus says, for instance —

> *"Assuredly, I say to you, there is no one who has left house or brothers or sisters or father or mother or wife or children or lands, for My sake and the gospel's, who shall not receive a hundredfold now in this time—houses and brothers and sisters and mothers and children and lands, with persecutions—and in the age to come, eternal life."* (Mark 10:29b-30, NKJV);

— He's not giving us licence for our families to bear the brunt of our self-interest. Nor is He telling us literally to abandon them, any more than "cut your hand off" or "pluck your eye out" are literal in Mark chapter 9, verses 43 and 47.

Rather, He's emphasising a point. He's urging us to make Him our greatest priority, above anything else that matters to us; to surrender to Him more fully and comprehensively than ever before, so He may take His rightful place as the CEO (or King, or Lord) of our business.

What needs sacrificing in each life is different for every person. We all value different things. But whatever we value more than Him needs to be brought into submission at His cross. For instance:

- Triumphalism is the counterfeit of living abundantly.
- Exercising control is the counterfeit of exercising Jesus' authority.[23]
- Willpower is the counterfeit of self-control.[24]
- Living with one foot in commercial practice and the other in Kingdom practice, is going to split us up the middle (see Matt. 6:24).

Jesus knows – and will reveal – what needs to be sacrificed by each of us. Even though Job was in the middle of a bitter complaint to God about His treatment of him, yet he still acknowledged God's indisputable trustworthiness:

> ***Though He slay me, yet will I trust Him.* (Job 13:15a, NKJV).**

Shadrach, Meshach and Abednego experienced a similar conviction in God's reliability, *whatever* the outcome of the appalling situation they faced as a result of Nebuchadnezzar's ego:

> *"...our God whom we serve is able to rescue us from the furnace of blazing fire; and He will rescue us from your hand, O king. But even if He does not, let it be known to you, O king,*

---

[23] Which we may do only in His Name, and only as He reveals how we may do so.

[24] The first being self-motivated, whilst the second is the fruit of Holy Spirit in us (see Gal. 5:22-23).

that we are not going to serve your gods nor worship the golden statue that you have set up." (Dan. 3:17-18, NASB).

Are you willing to embrace the same trust – sacrificing yourself for the Kingdom of Jesus, the Christ?

Business implications and application

How can a business express 'sacrifice'?

> As with every true sacrifice, something – or someone – dies: us! Our pride, reputation, and egos.

The only place to start, is for each of us to ask Jesus what He wants us to sacrifice. We have to start with ourselves. For instance:

- *We,* as business owners, choose to surrender to Jesus, rather than continuing to resist Him, defaulting to a 'wrestling back of control into our own hands'.
- *We* start putting our employees and suppliers (not just our customers – the ones we 'get something from') before ourselves.
- *We* may need to take no pay, whilst we ensure that our team earns their guaranteed wages.
- *We* may have to put in our last dollar, without seeing any return, before we see God come through.

My point is not to create new rules to live by, but to demonstrate that when we allow God to put His finger on anything and everything, we acknowledge His longing to impart far greater blessings to us, in their place. He's teaching us not only surrender, but also the need to exercise faith in Him.

So, how do we know when we *are* acting in faith, rather than out of misguided stubbornness, stupidity, or a rash attempt to manipulate Him into doing our will?

It all goes back to the vital importance of knowing our call,[25] which is *exactly* for moments like these. Without the confidence that *He's* called us into business, it's quite possible that we'll act presumptuously. But when we know, with a deep conviction (tested, weighed and agreed by trusted others) that we're fulfilling *His* call, then we can lay everything at the cross in confidence and trust.

And if we get it wrong? – Even then, we find He's still faithful and infinitely gracious to us (see 1 John 1:9).

Entrepreneur's Insights (Myself)

I'll never forget a year when I was seeking God for deeper insight. Twice, on different nights, He woke me at 3:00 a.m. – each time with the same question: "Son, will you give up everything for me?"

The first time, I replied, "By 'everything', what do you have in mind, Lord?"

He responded, "Will you give me every dollar and cent of your money – your home, savings, investments and retirement plan?" I can tell you, I wrestled!

---

[25] See chapter 3.

For nearly two hours I churned, argued, and dissembled. I realised that night, like never before, what a grip money had on me. Eventually, around 5:00 a.m., I agreed. I laid my wealth down at the cross. The visible evidence of my entire working life's efforts, accumulated for my family's future benefit – house, bank accounts, retirement savings, investments – all had to be written out of my control.

Yet what an emotional freedom it gave me! I'd had no idea what a weight I'd carried, grasping my money so protectively – a security-blanket that no one had been allowed to question, until that night.

The second time He woke me, I heard the same question in my head. I replied similarly: "What do you mean by 'everything' this time, Lord?"

"Will you give Me your reputation?" He answered.

This struggle was no easier than my first. To be fair, I'm not a media personality, so I don't have any public reputation to speak of. But I have pride and, with it, I had nurtured self-importance. Once more, therefore, I wrestled. "God, you've already got all my savings. How people perceive me allows me to generate my income. Are you really asking me to give up whatever creditability I've built up locally, and also my means of earning an income?"

There was a calm silence; God just waited for me to catch up. It was enough. He clearly meant, "I've asked you. You don't need Me to confirm it. I'm waiting for your answer, when you're ready."

It took me a slightly shorter time to get there this night — only 1½ hours instead of two. By 4:30 a.m., I was ready to lay what I thought of as 'my reputation' on His altar. "Lord, there is nothing and no one I want more than you," I told Him. "I'm not willing to give up my relationship with You for anything else; so yes, I give You my reputation. Do with it whatever You know is best."

For a second time, I felt a rush of emotional relief. I'd given up a second burden that I didn't even know I'd been carrying.

During that second night, I'd sensed He had a third question for me. I'd actually been wrestling with it during the same 1½ hours, even though it remained unspoken as yet. So I carried on: "While we're at it, Father, I know there's a third thing: You're going to ask me to give You my family also. So, yes, You can have them too. Whatever You see fit to do with them, or ask of them, I trust You completely. You're a far better Father than I will ever be! You want only to bless them; and that's far better than anything I can give them. Thank You for encouraging me to release them into Your safe keeping."

Until 12 months ago, He'd not asked me to take practical action in respect to my three commitments. I started holding each of those areas of my life very lightly; and, as He has now begun to claim 'in practice' what He'd already asked me to release to Him, I am finding they have less and less hold over me. I'm merely His caretaker: they're already no longer mine, but His.

Personal sacrifice is an inevitable part of our journey as Christian business owners — both emotional and practical. Until we embrace this, we'll find pain arising repeatedly in our businesses. Once we lay down voluntarily whatever He asks, God takes over — and it's an exciting journey from then on!

Dina's Story

I was born in Indonesia. At age 16, I was given an opportunity to surrender my life to Christ but told God I wasn't going to follow Him yet, "...but I probably will by the time I'm 30".

I found out that God holds us to our careless words! I'd just turned 30 and was at work one day when, out of nowhere, God spoke to me and said, "You told Me that, when you were 30, you'd follow Me. Now, write down what I tell you!"

I was aware that this was an invitation I'd regret deeply, if I turned it down. Looking back, it was a definite call.

Overnight, the focus, direction and motivation of my life all changed. I had no idea what following God looked like — but I knew I had to do it.

Shortly after, I had a dream telling me I should start a coffee business. No one ran an 'espresso'-style coffee business in Indonesia at that time. I started researching, even visiting Europe to check out Italian-style coffee bars.

Out of the blue, someone we knew contacted me. "I've bought a coffee roastery", he said. "Would you be interested in going into a coffee business with us?" My "yes" was instant!

My husband and I were already running one successful business at the time, so we were able to finance the new company. We set it up as a franchising business right from the start because we'd already recognised its growth potential.

Things started positively. We now had two franchise outlets underway and were about to open our third when personal circumstances altered for our business partners. The choices we faced were either to buy them out or sell our shares to them. Buying was our preference...but God gave us clear understanding that we must sell: "You have to let go of the business you've just started." Additionally, He told us to bless it as we left!

Emotionally, it cost us dearly, because we knew we'd started a winner; but He was testing our willingness to trust Him. Would we let go, and walk faithfully with Him? We did. And it's been a joy to watch from a distance what's happened to that business – it's still very successful: something we're proud of!

After a two-year restraint of trade period, I began formulating plans for a new coffee franchise company. As soon as we could, my husband and I started looking for a site, and opened our first, very successful, outlet in a large plaza in the city centre.

Little did we know that we were about to begin a 10-year 'wilderness journey'. In our second year, a family *member became very unwell, and we had to sell our first business, which we still owned at that time, to pay for their care. Putting it up for sale broke our hearts; it was our 'baby' — we'd been building it since early in our marriage. And we'd hoped it would give us a lifestyle income well into our retirement.*

So, we started an immediate franchise expansion of our new coffee business, opening a second store. Instantly we hit roadblocks and within three months, things started to go drastically wrong. Every interested party who was going to take up franchises, lost interest. We went for a whole year with zero income. The size of our existing sites was inadequate for the throughput that developed and the position of pillars in the middle of the stores created problems. And in addition to all this there were roadworks outside, which stopped foot traffic into our sites.

To combat these challenges, we acted proactively and opened a third outlet. But that year, the number of coffee businesses in that same street went from five to 12. Turnover in that outlet dived down.

Someone approached us and asked to become a fourth franchisee, in a site he'd found. We agreed but again hit serious problems. They pulled out just after we'd instigated the full internal fit-out. Fortunately we found another couple to take it on . . . but they were from overseas and, after a short trip back to their home country, the husband was told he couldn't return to Indonesia because he didn't have the correct visa. With just six weeks to sell, they did so as fast as they could, to the first person they found: someone who wouldn't take on a franchise. Because the overseas couple were no longer in Indonesia, we had no practical means to enforce their contract, so it lapsed, and we lost that franchise altogether.

At considerable personal disadvantage, we determined to honour God, and paid all fit out costs ourselves. Then we opened a different site — our second one in a mall.

Then, on September 5th 2011 an earthquake struck Indonesia. We lost all of our stores except the mall shops. But one wasn't being profitable, so we broke the lease (costing us the equivalent of US$207,000). Our second mall shop was the only part of our business making any money by now; but the mall management decided at that point, that they were going to put up our lease — by 100%.

So, that business was wiped off the map too, in addition to the one we'd already sold. The result was that we lost all the money we'd earned from 10 years of running businesses.

But along the way, we'd invested in some coffee roastery equipment and in premises in a local suburb where it had been housed. That's all we had left. It wasn't a franchise — just a supply company. But we started roasting and supplying. Amazingly, after all the years of pain and intense challenges and difficulties, over the 10 years since we started this business, it's grown into a thriving operation and our coffee is now sold throughout the country.

Through all these experiences, I began to understand something of God's strategy. Sometimes He gives us amazing experiences, with miracles taking place on all sides. These times are, I believe, to teach us that He's faithful, and to build our trust in Him. At other times, He requires a sacrifice from us that is absolute. Through it all, He was faithful.

Everything in my life was tested during those years. The very, very strong financial base we started with, all went, until we had no money left. God wanted us to give everything up to Him, in every single area of our life. For a long time, everything seemed dry, barren, utterly fruitless. Everything about my own identity was challenged too.

But we held on. God's faithfulness is now absolutely clear to me. He wants His children to experience Kingdom life. And to get me there, He wanted to run our current business, through me; and that could only happen through total sacrifice of everything I held dear; our family, money, time, effort, and energy.

As Scripture says:

> **...though now for a little while you may have had to suffer grief in all kinds of trials. These have come so that the proven genuineness of your faith—of greater worth than gold, which perishes even though refined by fire—may result in praise, glory and honor when Jesus Christ is revealed. Though you have not seen him, you love him...** (1 Pet. 1:6a-8a, NIV)

Dina
Business owner
(set in Indonesia)

Time-out, for Reflection:

- What sacrifices have you had to make in the past? Is there joy in them for you? If not, why not?
- What further sacrifices is He calling you to make now?
- What's the fruit of those sacrifices – in your life, the life of others, and/or in your business?
- What difficulties in business have been of your own making (e.g. failing/refusing to listen; taking or re-initiating control; not following His lead)? What will you and He do about those now?

CHAPTER 12
THE HOLY BUSINESS

> *...but as He who called you is holy, you also be holy in all your conduct, because it is written[26], 'Be holy, for I am holy.'*
> (1 Peter 1:15-16, NKJV).

> *I beseech you therefore, brethren, by the mercies of God, that you present your bodies a living sacrifice, holy, acceptable to God, which is your reasonable service.*
> (Rom. 12:1, NKJV).

Jesus' holiness wasn't a "holier than thou" morality. It was invitational truth. It didn't drive the crowds from Him; it drew them towards Him. And He longs to attract the world still, through us.

Holiness is deeply practical. Living a holy life unlocks the vibrant quality of life that Jesus made available to us through His death and resurrection. It's life-giving, not ritualistic. It enables our access to God's throne of grace, and also blossoms in us as the results of that access. It allows us to embrace and enjoy the life of Jesus, as our own. And that's utterly appealing!

---

[26] Quoted from Lev. 11:44.

I'd like to suggest a really simple, practical, workable description of what holiness is, both in respect to God and to mankind, as follows:-

- God is holy includes –
    - He's untainted by sin (Num. 23:19);
    - He's glorious (Exo. 15:11);
    - He's so perfect that He's terrifying (Heb. 12:21; Deut. 19:19), even lethal (Exo. 19:21), until we're reborn into the Kingdom of God, through Christ;
    - He's entitled to and worthy of all adoration and reverence, by every created being (Deut. 6:13; Luke 4:8).

    Jesus taught that God's awe-inspiring greatness is correctly understood only when we experience it alongside His intimate approachability. To emphasise either attribute, at the expense of the other, is to receive an imperfect revelation of Him:

    "Our Father . . . in Heaven; . . . hallowed be your Name." (Luke 11:2a, NKJV).

- We are holy includes –
    - We're set apart for God's purpose by His living presence in us (2 Cor. 5:17);
    - He's made a way available, through Jesus, for us to be truly 'one' with the Father, exactly as Jesus is (John 17:11);
    - By faith in Christ we've been attributed (Gal. 2:16), both the character (Gal. 5:22-23) and perfection (Matt. 5:48) of God, so the Father sees us exactly as He sees Jesus.

But how is it even possible for us to be holy?

Outside of Christ, it's not. Yet He commands us to *Be holy, as I am holy* – so, through Him, it is possible!

How, then, do we appropriate this beautiful gift of holiness?

Certainly not through our own efforts, but by faith alone . . . which, by the way, is another gift given by God, in His sovereignty, so no one has a right to boast about it (see Eph 2:8-9).

Our characters are changed into that of Jesus, by abiding in Him and His word (see John 15:4). As we do, His very nature transfers to us and we are –

> *...transformed into His image from glory to glory, just as from the Lord, the Spirit.* (2 Cor. 3:18b, NASB).

Why, then, are we told that <u>we</u> must put off the old self and put on the new? (see Eph. 4:17-24).

Because one of God's gifts to us is that we'll always have freedom to *choose*. His longing and intention is that we choose to cooperate with Him, in His ongoing process of transforming our character into the perfect nature of Jesus (see 2 Cor. 3:18). When we agree with Him, we are embracing our new self. As James put it:-

> *Therefore submit to God. Resist the devil and he will flee from you. Draw near to God and He will draw near to you. Cleanse your hands, you sinners; and purify your hearts, you double-minded. Lament and mourn and weep! Let your laughter be turned to mourning and*

> your joy to gloom. Humble yourselves in the sight of the Lord, and He will lift you up. (Jam. 4:7-10, NKJV).

Submission to God is thus revealed as a prerequisite for holiness: being set apart for God. It empowers us to resist whatever is not holy. Holiness is a priceless gift. It's beauty is that, through it –

- We grow a more attractive character and nature, becoming like Christ;
- We are fulfilled, not diminished;
- We are completed, not depleted.

When we perceive the truth of this, we find we have everything to gain and nothing to lose, by embracing holiness – including in business.

Will holiness involve sacrifice?

Absolutely! Have no doubt about that. But, as we grasp the extraordinary nature of His gift – the wealth of God's character in us (see Col. 1:27) – then what we might initially think we're leaving behind, fades into insignificance and becomes irrelevant.

Business implications and application

Holiness is one of God's core attributes (if not the core attribute), mentioned 850 times in the Old Testament alone[27]. That being the case, if we don't take holiness into our business, what *ought* we to take into it?

---

[27] *New Bible Dictionary*, (3rd Ed.,1996). Consulting Editors: IH Marshall, AR Millard, JI Packer, DJ Wiseman. Pub. Inter-Varsity Press, Leicester, England. p. 477.

> Your personal choices
> affect your business,
> and are reflected in
> your business life.

Let's pause for a moment and undertake a personal, and company, audit of our holiness.

Allow Holy Spirit both to convict and encourage you. What's your current experience of holiness? Ask Him to search and weigh you and your business, so you may receive grace. Where do you or your business not align with God's Truth? Allow Him gently to challenge and convict you:

- God – Father, Son and Holy Spirit
  Do you see Him as:
    - Present, reliable, a friend, an advocate, faithful, permission-giving, embracing, forgiving, gracious, kind, father-like, revealed, holy, merciful, approachable?

  Or, for instance, as:
    - Distant, unreliable, an enemy, accuser, unfaithful, permission-denying, austere, punishing, judging, unkind, absent, unfair, hidden, unrealistic, demanding, unapproachable?
- Your view of yourself:
  Do you see yourself as:
    - Forgiven, empowered, purified, loving, peaceful, patient, made worthy, reliable, gentle, trustworthy, made righteous, self-controlled, truthful, valued, ransomed, restored, friend?

  Or, for instance, as:
    - Alone, forgotten, abandoned, rejected, unforgiveable, sinful, unlovable, worried, unworthy, gossip,

grudge-holder, liar, emotionally-crippled, dirty, defensive, irrelevant to God?
- Your behaviours and speech:
  Do you see your attitudes and words as:
  - Generous, forbearing, forgiving, wholesome, understanding, concerned, faithful, dependable, fruitful, pure, loving, full of integrity, abiding in Christ?

  Or, for instance, as:
  - Mean, blame-shifting, judgemental, unfaithful, flirt, pornography-user, adulterer, unkind, arrogant, critical, excusing sin, unreliable, dishonest, manipulative, dominating, controlling, deceiving, jealous, unforgiving, sarcastic, unfruitful, defensive, avoiding Christ?
- Your company and team
  Does the company embrace and live out:
  - Truthfulness, generosity, diligence, people first, encouragement, honesty, service-without-offense, over-delivering, gentleness, forbearance, hope, love?

  Or is it, for instance, given to:
  - 'Dishonest scales'[28], disregard for others, pride, lies, half-truths, gossiping, laziness[29], sexual inuendo, undermining reputations, win-at-all-costs, under-delivery?

Do not be discouraged! Remember: Holy Spirit *never* condemns, He convicts. Conviction is always an invitation – He wants His best for you.

---

[28] See Prov. 11:1.

[29] See Prov. 6:9-10.

Entrepreneur's Insights (Samuel)

Christians want – expect – everyone to be nice; but sadly, they're not always! Be ready to deal with people who aren't ethical. Be both wise and gracious (Matt. 10:16, NKJV). Look to God alone for approval. Live only by His standards – integrity, grace, purity, holiness.

As a small business, we'd won a GB £250,000 contract from a government department. We engaged a team of consultants and began work. All went well for about six months. Then I was called into a meeting without warning, alone. There were 10 client staff in the room, including a lawyer. He regaled me with false accusations, claiming we were in breach of contract and that I'd been lying. It was intentional bullying without any evidence being presented. Their intention was to intimidate and demoralise me and it certainly upset me to be told I was unethical, because I strive to be known for straight dealing.

The client wanted to frighten us into giving up the contract so they could give it to someone else, as an act of nepotism, and it worked. I wasn't willing to take on a legal battle with them: they were too powerful. So, we paid off our contractors and walked away. It was very painful, and not just financially. My character had been impugned and I'd been intentionally humiliated.

But so, of course, was Jesus. He was subject to false charges at His trial, yet remained silent and true to Himself without retaliating, still loving His enemies.

Although we needed a little time to lick our wounds, we also knew that we'd walked away with our heads held high: we hadn't compromised our fundamental values.

If others attack your character or tell lies about you, don't fight back in the same way. There may be times when God gives us His sanction to defend our position; but as always with God, it's what's in our hearts that is the most important factor. When our motive is wounded pride or revenge, step back! Be true to yourself and God. He will approve you even when others don't.

Samuel
International consultant
(United Kingdom)

Entrepreneur's Insights (Myself)

I've had clients confess to me financial dishonesty, tax evasion, pocketed cash, personal expenses put through as business costs, extramarital affairs, pornography use and addiction, swearing, mistreatment of others, anger, and unforgiveness.

All of these will impact your business, and you personally. We can't escape our own conscience – nor the searchlight of the Holy Spirit. His specialty is shining a spotlight on our sin. His purpose is to restore our relationship with God, fully and completely.

Imagine a business conference where, as Christians, you and I are gathered to hear an expert speak on business improvement. As he does so, he comes under the anointing of the Holy Spirit and starts receiving words of knowledge about ways in which our businesses are ignoring and abusing holiness.

How will we respond to God?

My advice is this: Adopt God's holiness, comprehensively. Seek out trusted friends to support you or get professional help if you need it – but do it!

> **For if you live according to the flesh you will die; but if by the Spirit you put to death the deeds of the body, you will live.** (Rom. 8:13, NKJV).

That verse applies as much to our business practices, as it does to us in other areas of our lives.

God is looking to forge humility, deep in our hearts. Allowing Him to put to death those things that will otherwise result in our death (spiritually, if not physically) is counter-intuitively, a joy! As we surrender, receive His forgiveness, and begin to enjoy obedience, He responds with untold blessings. Whatever we sacrifice somehow loses its power over us, and becomes wonderfully irrelevant.

Stuart's Story

> I run a construction contracting company, in New South Wales, Australia. About 10 months ago, I lost one of my top foremen to a competitor. He was headhunted.
> I see my role as a 'maker of leaders'. My company is simply the vehicle through which I do that. I'd spent

years mentoring this man, developing his leadership skills. I thought we had a good working relationship . . . but he went for an interview and accepted the new job without even talking to me. When he handed me his notice, I was shocked and hurt. I asked why. "They've offered me more money", he replied, having the wisdom to be somewhat embarrassed. I was gutted.

After he'd left us, though, he added insult to injury by systematically attracting my best workers to his new employer. Nearly 10 left, over time.

A couple of months ago, one of those employees rang me, nervously, to say, "Boss, I've made a mistake. Would you take me back?"

I was still very sore, and replied "From anywhere else, maybe — but not from there. You know they're our major competitor. I've no time for anyone disloyal."

I hadn't yet recognised my response as unforgiving. I justified it, out of the hurt I felt.

Now, put that story 'on pause' if you will; and 'fast forward' with me, to a second, which was happening at the same time.

We'd had a fluctuating workload for two years, which made it difficult to keep my 45 staff fully occupied. I'd been looking forward expectantly, therefore, to our biggest and most loyal client giving us his latest package of work. For 25 years we'd enjoyed an exclusive relationship with them. No competitors, no tendering: just negotiated prices every time they gave us work. Our delivery and quality had always been 'best in class', and I kept it that way for a reason. I was therefore dismayed when they told me their next block of work (260 lots) would be tendered, and that they were including some out-of-town contractors in the tender process who I knew well: they regularly 'low-balled' their tenders, to buy work.

I experienced another sense of betrayal and confusion. Just as with the foreman who'd left, there'd been no discussion, no explanations, no warning.

To try to address the situation, I did everything I could, to show our commitment to them. I prepared the tender documents and prices personally, wanting our offer to be the best package we could make it, offering to deliver all 260 lots within just 32 weeks, which I thought would be attractive. They also asked us to submit the tender in two smaller parcels of approximately 130 lots each, which we did.

The review time was expected to be a week but seven days' later, I'd heard nothing. My concern grew. Had the other contractors bought the job by pricing low?

I met with a fellow business owner and friend, and told him both stories. He asked if I saw myself principally as a businessman, trying to show my Christianity through my values, or if I saw God's involvement in my business as being more than that. "The first", I replied. He responded with a challenge: "Then make God the CEO of your business, handing over all control to Him". He shared, from his own experience, how doing so had made a significant difference to his business. He also pointed out my unforgiveness towards my former employee, asking me: "How different would this be, do you think, if you rang up the foreman who's left you and said to him: 'I hold no ill-will towards you and in fact hope we can talk openly about what's happened. You've benefited from employing some of our good staff, so I wanted to ask if there was anyone else you'd like to have? If so, I'd be happy to speak to them and suggest they come your way'."

My jaw dropped. "I think I've got some praying to do," I replied, "and a new job description to write – for a CEO!"

I went back to my office, pulled out an old job description I'd written a while back, when we considered employing a CEO. I put God's Name at the top, printed it, signed it on His behalf, then scanned and emailed it to myself, as a symbol of my willingness for Him to take over the leadership of my business. I spent that weekend in prayer too, asking God to forgive my unforgiveness. Peace followed. I knew that, behind all this, He had a great plan brewing – all the shadow boxing and stress would change.

Within just three weeks, two extraordinary things happened:-

First, I was summoned to my client's HQ. The coffee and jovial banter boded well; until he turned to business. "Your price for the total project was OK", he said, "but the two 'halves' weren't competitive. Actually, we decided a while ago to get two other contractors to undertake the 260 lots (half each). I'm sorry: you won't be getting this work after all."

I was unable to contain my disappointment: it must have been written all over my face. Twenty-five years of loyalty gone in a stroke. No discussion, no opportunity to change his mind. But then, a mischievous smile spread across my client's face. He turned over a new plan, one I hadn't seen before, which showed a total of 700 lots. "This is the job I want your company to undertake," he said.

I went from 'zero' to 'ecstatic' in about two seconds! To miss out on the 260 had been horrible; but to be offered 700 – with no tender, just a negotiated price like always – was a work-continuity dream. It would keep my team employed for 24 months plus. No more fluctuating workload, and our working relationship was going to continue.

Then two weeks later, the foreman who'd left last year phoned me to say he'd realised he'd made a terrible mistake. He now understood the value of our leadership training programme. His new company had no interest in his personal growth, he said. He really wanted his job back, if I'd take him. This time I answered "Yes, on the condition that you phone all your former work colleagues here and apologise to them for showing poor leadership. That will restore relationships between you and them." He did, within 24 hours.

His current employer is now trying to persuade him to stay, so I don't actually know what the final outcome will be – but it no longer matters to me. I recognised the fingerprints of the Holy Spirit all over this: first, in my change of heart, then in his.

Not a bad performance appraisal for God's first three weeks in the job, as my new CEO!

The lessons for me, in this? –

1) *Holiness includes discipline:* Humble yourselves, therefore, under God's mighty hand, that He may lift you up in due time. (1 Pet. 5:6, NIV);
2) *And the requirement to forgive:* "But if you do not forgive others their sins, your Father will not forgive your sins." (Matt. 6:15, NIV);
3) *Surrender control to the Lord.* He is able to do immeasurably more than all we ask or imagine, according to his power that is at work within us. (Eph. 3:20, NIV).

Stuart
Company owner, construction contracting company
(set in Australia)

Time-out, for Reflection:

- How has holiness been encouraging and beautiful to experience?
- Read Psalm 51 – David's Psalm of contrition. Is there anything God is asking you to address? (Be encouraged: repentance brings freedom, and holiness.)
- Is there anyone you need to forgive (see Matt. 6:14-15)?
- Or of whom you need to ask forgiveness (see Matt. 5:23-24)?

- None of us can be holy without Jesus but in Him, holiness is a powerful and breathtaking result of His work of grace within us. Spend some time worshipping Him.

    Give to the Lord the glory due His name; Bring [yourself as] an offering, and come before Him. Oh, worship the Lord in the beauty of holiness! (1 Chron. 16:29, NKJV).

CHAPTER 13
THE ABUNDANT BUSINESS

"I have come that they may have life, and that they may have it more abundantly."
(John 10:10b, NKJV).

Yet you do not have because you do not ask. You ask and do not receive, because you ask amiss, that you may spend it on your pleasures.
(Jam. 4:2b-3, NKJV).

Three times I wanted to start writing this chapter. Three times God took me back to the previous one, *The Holy Business*. Two reasons became apparent:

- He had things to address in me; and
- He wants us all to be clear that His holiness, is an utterly positive experience.

We're unwise when we rush Christ's work. When we do, He simply takes us back to when we tried a shortcut. With each attempt to bypass Him, His discipline, born of grace, becomes more pronounced – until we either surrender or disregard His voice, searing our consciences.

- Surrender . . . Prepares us for blessing and abundant life.

- Turn a deaf ear . . . Well, then you're on your own: beware! You may get exactly what you've asked for: His silence and absence.

May I suggest, therefore, that if Holy Spirit hasn't yet finished speaking to you about holiness, you'd be better to stop reading, for now. Move back to prayer. Listen. Hear. Follow through on what He's showing you.

As we submit ourselves into His gracious care, we allow God to give us Jesus' character. We start thinking, wanting, and asking as Jesus does. Our desires stop flowing from self-interested motives and start to align with the mission of the King (see Luke 11:2 and Psa. 37:4).

Have you ever noticed the astonishing liberality with which abundance flows from God?

- He speaks matter out of absolutely nothing (Gen. 1: 3,6,9,11,14,20,24,26);
- He creates a universe so vast (Gen. 1:1) that it can't be fully investigated, known, or mapped (Job 38);
- He owns 'cosmic storehouses and farms', of *astonishing* wealth (Psa. 33:7; 50:10);
- He expresses extravagant generosity, daily (Psa. 51:12);
- He invents music as a brand-new art-form, then arranges for the stars to sing to Him (Job 38:7);
- He turns single units of production, into 40, 60 or 100 units, in just weeks (Mark 4:8);
- He multiplies food in outlandish quantities (2 Kings 4:1-7; Mark 6:30-44; Mark 8:1-9);
- He brings fruitfulness – not out of frenetic activity, but out of restful abiding (John 15:4);

- He rewards business faithfulness, with disproportionate promotion and bonuses (Luke 19:16-17);
- He restores every cell, nerve, muscle, sinew, bone, and system in dead bodies, to make them live again (1 Kings 17:17-24; Mark 5:22-43; Luke 7:11-17; John 11:32-45);
- He rewards even paltry sacrifices with multiplied returns, in both personal relationships and business assets (Matt. 19:29).

And all these are only the tiniest sample of the lavishness which He cascades onto us.

Paul lived daily under the awareness and experience of God's abundant supply. He also understood that it wasn't for his comfort primarily, but rather for God's glory:-

> *And my God shall supply all your need according to His riches in glory by Christ Jesus. Now to our God and Father be glory forever and ever. Amen* (Phil. 4:19-20, NKJV).

God showers abundance on us because He chooses to – not as an incentive for our compliance. It's an expression of His heavenly glory, revealed on earth. He's passionate about embracing everyone (we who know Him, and a world that doesn't yet) into the very same relationship He enjoys Himself, within the Trinity (see John 17:20-21).

We don't have to be perfect before receiving from Him: perfection belongs to Jesus alone. His gift of abundance is one expression of His grace, given not as compensation for works-based obedience, but because He wants it so.

Abundance follows surrender (read John 10:10 in the context of the preceding verses 1–9). Surrender is an act of obedience that results in the gift of holiness being formed in us. Difficulties arise when our egos decide they don't wish to surrender. Yet surrender we must, if we truly long to participate in His most intimate expressions of abundance, because there are conditions, e.g. –

> *If you abide in Me, and My words abide in you, you will ask what you desire, and it shall be done for you.* (John 15:7, NKJV);
>
> *But without faith, it is impossible to please Him, for he who comes to God must believe that He is, and that He is a rewarder of those who diligently seek Him.* (Heb. 11:6, NKJV);
>
> *Yet you do not have because you do not ask. You ask and do not receive, because you ask amiss, that you may spend it on your pleasures.* (Jam. 4:2-3, NKJV).

Business implications and application

I understand why we'd want abundance – who wouldn't? But what's the point of surrendering to Christ, to get it? After all, being a Christian doesn't guarantee business profitability: non-Christians build and own profitable businesses too, using their own capitalist methodology. Similarly, being a Christian doesn't guarantee immunity from failure or liquidation. Christian businesses fail in the same way that non-Christian businesses do.

But the point is, as Robert put it to me (he tells his fuller story later):

I know there are a lot of very successful people who don't believe in God. But the one thing I have which they don't, is that I wake up with a hope and satisfaction so deep it has nothing to do with money; I wake up with a relationship so powerful that it means far more to me than anything else on this earth. If God took my business away from me completely, then I know for sure that He's got something bigger planned! I'm not afraid, and I hold on lightly, not tightly, to everything He's asked me to oversee for Him.

Another way of putting it, is this:

> Abundance means so much more than success.
> Business *success* is measured in profit, value, money, and material gain.
> *Abundance* is a gift of Jesus, drawing us into an adventure of faith with Him!

God's abundance is intended to cover every area of our life, not just the few the corporate world aims for, skewed by society's values. Here's a sample of what Jesus offers – you could add many more:-

- General thriving and health;
- A genuine love for others;
- Creativity;
- New product and service inspirations;
- New and improved ways of doing life or business;
- Peace of mind and of heart;

- Provision, financial and otherwise;
- Referrals, and business that come out of the blue;
- New relationships, to help us build our lives and businesses;
- Outstanding and loyal staff;
- Problem-solving, with all of God's resources at our disposal;
- Knowing God's presence alongside us;
- Dreams and prophetic words that speak into our situations.

Our choice is: will we follow Him His way, or won't we? If we do, then we have Jesus' words to rely on:-

> *But seek first the kingdom of God and His righteousness, and all these things shall be added to you.* (Matt. 6:33, NKJV).

Does that sound naïve? If it does, are you surprised? For —

> *...God chose the foolish things of the world to shame the wise* (1 Cor. 1:27a, NIV).

Do you remember the battles of ancient Israel, which we looked at in chapter 4? Not to put too fine a point on it, God's instructions were absurd, if viewed from the perspective of military strategy. Yet the fact is that every time they relied on their relationship with Him (and His with them), asking for and obeying His plan for that specific occasion, they won; and each time they didn't, they lost.

Will we believe, and apply that faith in heartfelt obedience? God's abundance can't be achieved the world's way.

Entrepreneur's Insights (Tracey)

I'm learning more and more to operate out of a place of peace – and for me, that's been radical. I've seen business owners encourage teams to hustle others, pushing them to buy what they may not need. It always seems to be an indication of the owner's personal insecurity or financial need.

Hebrews 4:11 talks about striving to enter the rest. It's about trusting God. He's the One who supplies our needs and arranges business deals if we align with Him. He knows where and how and when we need to fish, far better than we do (Luke 5:4 and John 21:6).

Tracey Olivier
Business Coach, Facilitator, Consultant and Author
https://www.traceyolivier.com
(South Africa / New Zealand)

Entrepreneur's Insights (Judy)

We studied the making of money in the Bible and noted that the making of it, in itself, is never a problem to God nor wrong; however, how we make it and what we do with it are important.

Set up your systems to respect people; to honour everyone involved. It's not just about money – it's about the respect of everything and everyone: shareholders, employees, clients, the environment, sustainability, etc. Business isn't just about maximising profit – it's about playing your part to help bring in the Kingdom of God, and that involves working in ways that bring wholeness and "Shalom" to everyone involved. These are aspects of Abundance.

God honours the giving of money too – it's like planting seeds. There was a time when we had no money, yet our attitudes and decisions were ruled by money. So, from the start of our business, we've consistently given from the business, both regularly and at the end of each project. And we also give personally, from our salaries, which the business pays to us. Don't justify not giving, by saying you're waiting until you're making good profits before you start giving. Give as an act of faith.

We pay our bills early rather than waiting until the last possible date. We want to develop wholesome relationships, because good business depends on relationships that last a long time.

Finally, respect yourself. Most of us limit ourselves because of a limited self-image. (You will make decisions in every area of your life which are a function of your own self-image). It is not prideful to invest in yourself as a child of God and become everything He has made you to be. Live life with deep confidence, based on who God created you to be and who you are in Christ – yet without having an ego.

Judy
International consultant
(United Kingdom)

Robert's Story

After an eventful career in the army, during which I served two tours in Iraq among many other things, I returned to civilian life, becoming the assistant director of Psychiatric and Medical Services for The University of Texas Medical Branch.

Time came when an attorney asked me if I'd consider becoming certified as a Legal Nurse Consultant, and review cases for their law firm. I'd never even thought of doing anything like that – or of having my own business; but after meeting them, then praying with my wife, we believed it was the right next step, so I studied for and became a Certified Legal Nurse Consultant, starting my own company – now, by God's grace, well-known and -respected in its field.

Shortly after we started the business, when business was still slow because we weren't yet well known, we got to know about someone who needed cash. I told my wife, Jerusha, that I felt very strongly we should give as much as we could. She was concerned because all our suppliers were due to be paid and, after doing so, we would have only $100 left over. I was convinced we should give $60 to the lady – leaving only $40 for us to live on. But after we talked and prayed, Jerusha said, "OK, let's do what you think we should." That night, I went out and gave our gift of $60.

The following morning at exactly 8 a.m., my phone started ringing . . . and it simply didn't stop! Call after call came in. Every call was a case being given to me. After the sixth case, my wife looked at me and said,

"Do you realise — God's given you one case for every $10 you gave away!" . . . Then she added with a smile, "Why didn't you give the full $100?"!

We've experienced so many instances of God's supply like that. He's never stopped giving us one blessing after another in our business — key people, new contracts, new ideas, new training, and opportunities to bless others. Every client I talk to, I ask if I can pray for them, whatever their medical issues. Most aren't Christians, but when I ask permission, I've never once been turned down. People are really open to the gentleness of God, expressed through His children.

The way we're seen in the public provides a satisfaction of knowing that God's in control. People know we're a Christian company and very different from any other company that does what we do.

Jerusha often says, "All we have to do is pray and God will take care of it." I don't worry. I believe that if we give everything over to Jesus, at the foot of the Cross, He'll take care of it, and us.

He also says "Yet you do not have because you do not ask. (Jam. 4:2, NKJV)" - so I keep asking! And you know what? I've never 'lost' anything without Him replacing it with something better — every time! When He shuts a house door, He opens a barn door.

But there's a condition too — I know I must stay faithful and committed to Him. I'm aware of Job's testing in the Old Testament; I've never experienced that level of testing and, to be honest, I hope I never do. But, to the level I have been tested, up till now, I've always found Him to be absolutely faithful. His abundance shines through, every time.

Robert Malaer
Malaer Legal Nursing Consulting, LLC
http://malaerlegalnurseconsulting.com
(United States)

Time-out, for Reflection:

- Do you relate to Judy's comment, *There was a time when we had no money . . . yet we were ruled by money?* If so, what needs to change?
- Do either of the statements in the following verse apply to you or your business?

  Yet you do not have because you do not ask. You ask and do not receive, because you ask amiss, that you may spend it on your pleasures. (Jam. 4:2b-3, NKJV).

- Have you positioned yourself to receive God's abundance? If not, will you choose to now?
- How does (or will) your business show abundance to others? Spend some time praising God for His faithful word.

CHAPTER 14
THE TRANSFORMING BUSINESS

> *But we all, ...looking...at the glory of the Lord, are being transformed into the same image from glory to glory, just as from the Lord, the Spirit.*
> (2 Cor. 3:18, NASB).

> *And do not be conformed to this world, but be transformed by the renewing of your mind, so that you may prove what the will of God is, that which is good and acceptable and perfect.*
> (Rom. 12:2, NASB).

Everything we've talked about so far has been about transformation – *our* transformation as individuals; and along with that, the transforming of our *businesses* into expressions of Jesus' Kingdom. It's a lifelong process.

Our journey may begin something like this. We start our Christian walk with amazement and gratitude for God's acceptance and forgiveness, through Jesus. Initially, it's easy to worship and honour Him. Our gratitude flows freely.

As we continue, we usually receive knockbacks and discouragements. The tendency, then, is for us to try to conform Him to *our* image and expectations, instead of what needs to happen: us being conformed to *His* – the image of

His Son (see Rom. 8:29). It pays to be alert to this change, for we're at risk of creating modern-day idols: mental understandings of God as we think He ought to be or want Him to be, rather than as He's revealed that He is. If you've done this, repentance is needed. He's gracious when we humble ourselves to Him. It's part of His process of transformation.

But there's still further change to go. As Paul wrote to the Corinthians:-

> *Brothers and sisters, I could not address you as people who live by the Spirit but as people who are still worldly—mere infants in Christ. I gave you milk, not solid food, for you were not yet ready for it. Indeed, you are still not ready. You are still worldly. For since there is jealousy and quarrelling among you, are you not worldly? Are you not acting like mere humans?* (1 Cor. 3:1-3, NIV).

Maturity comes through our choices. As we embrace God's awe-inspiring transformation of us, its outworking creeps up on us almost unnoticed. It's as if we wake up one day and find that –

- We *want* to lay our lives down at the Cross;
- We *want* what He wants, infinitely more than whatever we once wanted;
- The pursuit of happiness gives way – beautifully – to the pursuit of holiness.

As Holy Spirit changes us, it should be natural and inevitable (unless we resist) for our businesses to change with us. Our lights shine. Jesus becomes the One whom people see, and they're drawn to Him:

> *"I am the light of the world. He who follows Me shall not walk in darkness, but have the light of life."* (John 8:12, NKJV).

How? Because we lay down our lives and take up His. We progressively become images of Him, doing what He did. As Jesus said:

> *"You are the light of the world".* (Matt. 5:14a, NKJV).

Business implications and application

Jesus announced His transforming mission by quoting Isa. 61:1-2a. Transformation, He confirmed, comes about through the Person, Presence and Power of Holy Spirit:-

> *"The Spirit of the Lord is upon Me, because He anointed Me to preach the gospel to the poor. He has sent Me to proclaim release to the captives, and recovery of sight to the blind, to set free those who are oppressed, to proclaim the favorable year of the Lord."* (Luke 4:18-19, NASB 1995).

Reforming the world wasn't mere talk to Jesus. He lived it practically. He and Holy Spirit went to work together, healing, delivering, performing miracles, multiplying physical resources, raising dead people to life, and demonstrating Father's sovereignty over both the natural and spiritual worlds.

Our businesses can be transformed into similar expressions of His mission. Because, remarkably, whether it makes us nervous or excited, we're called and equipped to follow in His footsteps:

> *For to this you were called, because Christ also suffered for us, leaving us an example, that you should follow His steps.* (1 Pet. 2:21, NKJV).

We are to do exactly what He did, bringing transformation to others' lives, in the same ways that He did.

He learned obedience to the Father's will (see Phil. 2:5-11). We are therefore also to yield willingly to His CEO-ship (Kingship) – so He can live through us, changing us in the process. When that happens, circumstances and people will find themselves drawn to His grace and plans. They will be blessed by them, even when they don't yet know it or recognise Him. This is our God of grace!

Any business built on a foundation other than Jesus' love and righteousness, becomes a pale substitute of what it's intended to be or capable of being. Substitutes are neither powerful, nor attractive, nor transformational.

Jesus is.

Jesus restored servants into friends (see John 15:15). Businesses have the opportunity, under His leadership, to transform lives, communities, towns, even countries.
This is no recent assertion. A group of German-speaking

Christians fled Moravia[30], in 1722, to escape persecution. Count Nicolaus Ludwig van Zinzendorf gave them land to settle on, on his estate in Herrnhut, Saxony. The Moravians began a 24/7 prayer meeting[31] which lasted over 100 years. As they prayed, they spread across the globe as missionaries, yet with a difference. They quickly realised that business gave them legitimacy and credibility in host countries. They became so convinced in the value of business as a means of gaining a foothold for the gospel, that they eventually refused to start a mission anywhere in the world, if they could not form businesses in the countries to which they went. Many businesses they started still exist and are responsible for many social services and reforms in those countries, as well as leading many to Christ. For them, business *is* mission.

Thus, not only are our businesses transformed into expressions of Jesus' mission; they also become vehicles through which God brings about "Isaiah 61-type" transformation to individuals and societies, who don't yet know Him. As recipients of Jesus' mission, businesses become missional themselves.

> **As we are transformed by Christ, He calls us into business, where He is the CEO (King). Through business, we bring transformation to others, through Christ.**

---

[30] In central Europe, now part of the Czech Republic.
[31] See https://www.christianitytoday.com/history/issues/issue-1/prayer-meeting-that-lasted-100-years.html

Entrepreneur's Insights (Peter & Juliet)

It's very important in business not to have an ego. When our egos take over, we stop listening to God – and that's the biggest downfall of all.

Allow others to fill in for your weaknesses, rather than feeling threatened by the fact that they may be better than you.

We have a long way to fall if customers suddenly desert our businesses. But it should never be our first priority to make customers happy: we should first build a relationship with our staff, make them feel truly valued, ensuring that they're happy in their work: then they'll make your customers happy.

The focus of business, for us, isn't primarily about making money. That just seems to happen on the more important things. What we aim for is contented staff, then satisfied customers, with a fantastic work environment, great shopping/café experience, and strong relationships with both.

Part of my (Juliet's) personal change is to become wiser and more tolerant, in handling both circumstances and people. I no longer take issues personally, so can therefore encourage my staff to be more steady emotionally. That brings about change in our business – and through the business, in customers.

All our staff know we're Christians and are running our business under the Lordship of Christ. Although most aren't Christians themselves, they feel safe. That's been transformational in our business. It's also transformed other businesses because we train our staff for leadership but sometimes we can't give them the roles they deserve; so we applaud them if they find something else that suits them well, and they want to move on to another company. In that way, we 'seed' transformed and transformational leaders, into other businesses around New Zealand, and sometimes even overseas.

Peter & Juliet Worsp
Terra Viva Home & Garden Ltd
(https://garden.terraviva.nz)
Terra Viva Café Ltd (https://cafe.terraviva.nz)
(New Zealand)

Rob's Two Stories

The Moravians[32]

In April 1758, 30 cash strapped Moravian Missionaries were sent to Suriname, a small country on the north coast of South America, bordered by the Atlantic Ocean to the north, Guyana to the west, Brazil to the south, and French Guiana to the east. They also brought a cargo of striped linen, having been inspired by Moravian businessman, John P. Weiss.

Weiss saw business both as a means of offering opportunities for Christian witness, and making profit – important for missionaries with no other means of

---

[32] Adapted from https://b4blessing.com/blog/2017/01, as well as a private article.

support. His business brain and passionate heart for the unsaved laid a foundation for what has become more than 260 years of what he called 'missionary commerce'.

Weiss's approach resulted in a transformative endeavour that truly entered the warp and woof of the fabric of Suriname society. Christians practicing their faith in the daily affairs of the marketplace were then, and still are for us today, a powerful example to Christian business, as it can undoubtedly be missional. It provided an entry point to the very heart of the Suriname community.

They founded Kersten & Co., (https://kersten.sr) in 1768, a company whose activities branched into key growth areas of Suriname's economy including mining, infrastructure, and tourism. Now, the group accounts for more than 1% of Suriname's total annual exports. As one of the oldest trade companies in the Western Hemisphere, Kersten has always been able to pride itself upon the trust of the community.

Through their faith-based commercial approach, a community-centric focus, and the care they shared especially for their workers, not only did they grow a thriving company, but their business became the base and nucleus for the group's largest and strongest congregations. By 1926 there were 13,000 members worshipping in seven church buildings, the largest Moravian congregation in the world. All related to the power and depth of the commercial approach.

Cadburys (a precis of the book "Chocolate Wars")[33]

Like the Moravian's before him, the brothers George and Richard Cadbury (founders of the Cadbury Chocolate empire) were men whose faith in God dictated every decision they made.

For the Christian capitalists of the 19th century, among whom the Cadbury's featured large, wealth creation was held to be a benefit for all stakeholders: workers, local community, and society at large. For them, business decisions were guided by the goal of spiritual wealth. Business ownership included a deep sense of social responsibility.

The Cadbury brothers' ideas were radical. Their factory was much more than a business to them: it was 'an opportunity to improve society', a living illustration more powerful than words. They conceived and built an entire new village, called Bournville, (moving the factory into it in 1879 (see https://en.wikipedia.org/wiki/Bournville). Forty years later, in 1919 a study compared children aged 6-12 from Bournville, with those brought up in Floodgate, a slum area of Birmingham. The former averaged 2-3 inches taller and 8 pounds heavier; and infant mortality was half that of Floodgate.

George and Richard's ideas were heavily influenced by their father, John. In the 1820's he'd been outraged by society's indifference to the plight of the poor. His was an era in which children as young as five were used as chimney sweeps, or carted off from

---

[33] *Chocolate Wars*, Copyright © 2011 Deborah Cadbury, Pub. Harper Press 77-85 Fulham Palace Road, Hammersmith, London, UK

the 'poor workhouses' to work in cotton mills and mines, as if disposable. Others died of neglect by their drunken parents. There were even accounts of children being killed by their parents, their clothes sold for a pittance to buy more gin.

George and Richard felt deeply moved by God to bring about change. Their development of drinking chocolate as a key product line, was itself driven by a wish to provide a 'healthy alternative' to cheap gin.

The altruistic business objectives of these and other 19th century Christians, and the spirit of their businesses, appear out of place in our 21st century shareholder capitalism with its seemingly exclusive focus on shareholder dividends and executive incomes. But they were just as out of place in their own day, treading a 'narrower path'. Their love of God, head for business, and heart for people wrestled with the issues of their day, transforming their communities and their nation.

Adapted from two articles compiled by Rob McArthur
Used with permission
Missional Business Advocate
(New Zealand)

Time-out, for Reflection:

- How is Holy Spirit already transforming your business? Staff? Customers? Suppliers?
- What further surrender does Jesus need, in order to continue its transformation, *from glory to glory* (2 Cor. 3:18, NASB)?
- Is it time to give Him praise and thanksgiving, alongside prayer?

Be anxious for nothing, but in everything by prayer and supplication, with thanksgiving, let your requests be made known to God; and the peace of God, which surpasses all understanding, will guard your hearts and minds through Christ Jesus. (Phil. 4:6-7, NKJV).

CHAPTER 15
THE RESOURCING BUSINESS

And God is able to make all grace abound toward you, that you, always having all sufficiency in all things, may have an abundance for every good work.

(2 Cor. 9:8, NKJV).

Then Isaac sowed in that land, and reaped in the same year a hundredfold; and the Lord blessed him.

(Gen. 26:12, NKJV).

Is God limited? If not, why do we so often behave as though He were?

For instance, have you ever decided to resource someone else's life, ministry or business out of your *lack*, rather than from a surplus you've decided is available for your giving – your 'disposable income'? True – to do so without God's prompting might risk being presumptuous; but what if it's not? What if He's waiting for you to step out in faith? Are you ready, if He does prompt you? (Jesus admires and applauds just such circumstances in Mark 12:41-44).

Or how do you feel about giving when you 'just know' that your offering is so meagre as to be pointless? (Again, Jesus receives enthusiastically just such a gift, bringing extreme resources out of the young giver's virtual nothingness – see Matt. 14:17-21).

Or have you ever given so liberally that it was excessively more than what was needed? (A very large group of enthusiastic believers did so in Exo. 36:2-7 – and their generosity was so extreme they had to be commanded to stop!)

When we've chosen in the past not to resource others, has it been because we couldn't see how God would resource us in return? This was one of the many issues faced by the Samaritan woman who met Jesus at the well. When Jesus asks for a drink, she shows a natural surprise that He, a Jew, would speak to her at all; to which Jesus responds that He can give her 'living water'. Misunderstanding Him, she replies:

> *"Sir, You have nothing to draw with, and the well is deep. Where then do You get that living water?"* (John 4:11, NKJV).

How many times have we questioned Him, or missed opportunities to give, because we couldn't see 'the bucket' – the invisible resources of Christ's Kingdom? The lack of a bucket only becomes a problem when we think it's the solution[34]. But why should it be? God alone is our provider (see Gen. 22:14) and the extravagant supplier of every need we will ever have (see Phil. 4:19).

---

[34] I'm indebted to my close friend and church pastor, Johno Melville, for sharing this perceptive insight from this story.

> The idea of 'disposable income' is a first world mindset-problem, even among Christians: We believe more in our lack, than in God's abundant surplus.

God tells us that *everything* we own, and earn, is His; therefore it's *all* disposable, at His sole instigation. We must hold it lightly.

When I was 19 or 20, I first read, *Rees Howells: Intercessor*[35]. It's one of the five most challenging books I've ever read. Born in 1879 in Wales, UK, Rees was converted during 1904, as the Welsh Revival was underway. Holy Spirit offered him a life of incredible blessing if he would surrender and obey Him in everything. One principle God told him to follow with money, early on, was that whatever need came first was to be the thing he spent on, or gave to. He was also never to ask for money from anyone else, nor let anyone know when he had a financial need. He was to operate exclusively by faith, in regard to his finances, with no one knowing.

Marrying in 1910, he and his wife were called to overseas mission. A week before they sailed, the mission organisation sent them money for the train fare to London, but Rees and his wife still needed provisions to take with them. Applying their principle, they spent their train fares to kit themselves out. By the time their train left next morning, they only had 10 shillings in their pockets. Their only option was to buy a ticket for as far as they could go, just 20 miles from their

---

[35] *Rees Howells: Intercessor*, Copyright © 1952 Norman Grubb, Pub. CLC Publications, CLC International (UK), Unit 5, Glendale Avenue, Sandycroft, Flintshire, CH5 2QP, UK

home, to the station where they had to change trains. There they went out to breakfast with friends, then walked back to the station, still with no money for the ongoing fare.

Rees heard the inner voice of Holy Spirit talk to him: "What would you do, if you had the money?" – "I'd get in the ticket queue and buy our next tickets," Rees replied. "Then that's what you should do," came the answer. Rees stood in the ticket queue, waiting to be served, twelfth in line. When he was second from the front, a man rushed up to him from the crowd roundabout, and thrust 30 shillings into his hand – enough to pay for their ongoing fares. It was only after this test, when they had already bought their tickets, that their breakfast friends also gave them additional financial gifts. He and his wife apparently sang all the way to London, where the missionary organisation gave them another £50 which they hadn't wished to send by post![36]

It's this same example of the faith Paul talks about:

> *But this I say: He who sows sparingly will also reap sparingly, and he who sows bountifully will also reap bountifully. So let each one give as he purposes in his heart, not grudgingly or of necessity; for God loves a cheerful giver. And God is able to make all grace abound toward you, that you, always having all sufficiency in all things, may have an abundance for every good work. As it is written: -- "He has dispersed abroad, He has given to the poor; His righteousness endures*

---

[36] This story is told in full, in chapter 23 ("Standing in the Queue") of *Rees Howells: Intercessor,* on pp. 158-164 of the 2016 paperback reprint.

> *forever." -- Now may He who supplies seed to the sower, and bread for food, supply and multiply the seed you have sown and increase the fruits of your righteousness, while you are enriched in everything for all liberality, which causes thanksgiving through us to God.* (2 Cor. 9:6-11, NKJV).

If we honestly believe that God has an infinite supply, what could stop us from resourcing others with the Kingdom's supplies, regardless of the cost to ourselves? Are we not the ones supposedly with the faith to receive God's provision for ourselves, in return? Could it be that God is challenging us, as business owners, to supply the needs of others, who don't yet have such faith?

Business implications and application

Businesses are part of the supply-chain in God's economy. As business owners, we need to be available for Him, through us, to provide for others' needs, as He points them out to us.

Paul assures us in 2 Cor. 9:8 that as we give, in obedience to God's prompting, we will receive back *far, far more* than we have given away. It's a principle that's spanned all of time. It started well before the Law of Moses (see Gen. 26:12, where Isaac experienced God's lavish provision), and has never stopped.

We are even told specifically by God to test Him regarding His ability and willingness to supply liberally for us (see Mal. 3:8-10).

Time and again, God speaks of His abundant supply. He's determined that we *mustn't* see Him as a grudging or incapable Giver. Rather, let's be 'hilarious' in our enjoyment and privilege of being allowed to give (see 2 Cor. 9:7).

Here are just four of the many hundreds of encouragements God gives us through Scripture, by which we can share His nature as a bountiful Giver[37]. Business is one of the ways that God's supply to others is activated – and we, as business owners, are invited to enjoy the miracles that result from this aspect of Kingdom living.

> *Honor the Lord with your possessions, and with the firstfruits of all your increase; so your barns will be filled with plenty, and your vats will overflow with new wine. (Prov. 3:9-10, NKJV);*
>
> *The generous soul will be made rich, and he who waters will also be watered himself. (Prov. 11:25, NKJV);*
>
> *He who has pity on the poor lends to the Lord, And He will pay back what he has given. (Prov. 19:17, NKJV);*
>
> *Give, and it will be given to you: good measure, pressed down, shaken together, and running over will be put into your bosom. For with the same measure that you use, it will be measured back to you." (Luke 6:38, NKJV).*

---

[37] For a list of 100, refer to https://www.openbible.info/topics/giving_to_the_needy

Entrepreneur's Insights (Alistair)

Some tips to cooperate with God, as a resourcer of others:-

- ***Trust God*** *– He can bring a spring of water even in a desert place.*
- ***Ask God to Increase your Faith*** *– We need to grow in faith, in order to be trustworthy with more Kingdom resources.*
- ***Be Available*** *– Both to God, and for God. Ask Him to break you, use you and mould you into His Presence. We can be so busy being busy, that we don't make time, to take time, with God. Don't let that be you.*
- ***Be Teachable*** *– Gather trusted, God-hearing mentors. Don't be defensive when they challenge you. Be faithful to hear the word of God, so you can grow in faith and character.*
- ***Conduct Precedes Character*** *– How do you deal with your finances? How do you treat your spouse? Are you what you say you are 'on the tin'? Find and work with people of good character, stable, open, and who display fruit. Get to know the heart of the person. Avoid those who blow their own trumpet.*
- ***Be Faithful, Trustworthy, Reliable, Credible*** *– Will you make only honest deals? Will you be true to God, yourself and others? When you commit to something, will you keep your word, even at disadvantage to yourself?*
- ***Be Intimate*** *– Giving yourself to others is just as important as giving material possessions or money. Be vulnerable with your emotions. Tell*

> people when you're having tough times. Your transparency, like that of Christ, will draw people in.
> - **Dare to Dream with God** – It helps you keep your vision bright and fun. Dream about what your business can be, and what resources you're willing to handle for the Kingdom. Go out and pray for people – watching God move and speak through you, will encourage you like little else.

Al Whitmoor-Pryer
Serial entrepreneur, International
Trainer & Business Developer, and Author
Asher Care Ltd & Kahanah Care Ltd
http://www.ashercare.co.uk
(United Kingdom)

Stewart's Story

In 1984, we bought a very run-down trading outlet. It wholesaled curtain tracks and product, later adding vertical blinds and venetians to our range, along with a measuring, quoting, and installing arm for curtains.

We committed to follow Jesus in all of our business dealings. If He told us to do something, that's what we'd do. One example of this was in our giving.

God blessed the business from its first year, and it started to grow visibly. We began earning more than we needed, from added income-streams, and the workload soon became more than we wanted to handle on our own. That's when we heard of a man who'd just been made redundant and was finding it difficult to get another job. After prayer, we became convinced we should give away the curtain fitting business to him, together with all the tools, ladders, and equipment he'd need to run that side of the business; which we did. Meanwhile the remainder of our business grew again under the blessing of God – and he did well with his new business also.

We paid ourselves salaries from the business, and we tithed these. But a moment came when I believed we should give from the business in addition to our personal giving. My wife and I prayed separately about how much we should give, and we both heard the same sum. So, that's what we gave, for one year.

Twelve months later, we went back to the Lord, asking if we should continue giving from the business for another year. Once again, He said yes; and once again we prayed independently. For a second time, we both heard exactly the same amount.

The third year the same thing happened. Then, in the fourth year, He told us to stop. We obeyed, as before.

During this time, a strange thing happened. People began to drop off, at our warehouse, all sorts of household furniture that they – and we! – didn't need. We had no idea why it was happening, but decided to wait and see. We found a place to store it on our business premises. It wasn't long before we started hearing about people who needed furniture – and we were able to supply it. This little reserve of couches, chairs, tables, etc, kept coming and going for several years. We helped a large number of people with free furniture. God had sovereignly organised His own resource centre, through our business!

In addition to furniture and our financial gifts, we also gave away a considerable number of new curtain tracks to a Christian organisation, starting a retreat centre. Again, our business was being used by God as a source of blessing to others.

Of course, this had a financial impact on us – one that we noticed. We had ample opportunity to agree to cash deals with some customers, as a number requested that we offer cheaper prices if they paid cash. We recognised this for what it was – a temptation to abandon God's values of holiness and righteousness. We chose not to succumb. There was a hidden cost to this decision because a few customers chose not to do business with us if we wouldn't discount for cash. The pressure to follow the wrong path intensified. Yet we knew that, because we wanted Jesus to be in charge, our business must operate completely honestly; so all sales continued to go through our books. Over time, God showed His favour on our choice to obey, and the blessings we received far outweighed the loss of the few cash sales. He blessed us resoundingly.

Being honest with our financial records brought a notable material benefit when we came to sell the business in 1994. The full value of our turnover and profit were transparently recorded, increasing the company's value.

But much more than that, to us, was the fact that we could sell with clean hearts, knowing we'd honoured

God and treated His business with integrity. And through our years in business, we'd been instrumental in blessing many in the community around us.

Stewart McLellan
Former director of Tracks and Tapes Limited
(New Zealand)

Time-out, for Reflection:

- In what ways can you remember God's extravagance towards you, your family, and your business? Thank Him.
- Ask Him to weigh your attitudes and actions regarding your resources (money, time, belongings, etc). How will you respond, as He reveals your heart, to you?
- What is God asking from you, through this discipleship challenge?:

    Freely you have received, freely give. (Matt. 10:8b, NKJV).

- Ask Him to help you change whatever attitudes need changing, so that you and your business may share the joy of resourcing the lives of others from hereon – in every way He shows you.

CHAPTER 16
THE UNLIMITED BUSINESS

The Lord's lovingkindness indeed never ceases, for His compassions never fail. They are new every morning; great is Your faithfulness.
(Lam. 3:22-23, NASB 1995).

...for God gives the Spirit without limit.
(John 3:34b, NIV).

With God, nothing is impossible. (Luke 1:37, NKJV).

So affirms the angel sent to Mary; and Jesus Himself reaffirms the same statement (see Matt. 19:26 and Mark 10:27).

I love how that message in Luke's verse doesn't say *"For God..."*, but rather *"With God..."*. Yet again, God displays His own personality and nature in His incredible invitation to Kingdom life: 'Do this with Me, Mary – I'll supply the power and make it happen, if you'll embrace the call of faith.'

In an earlier visitation, with similarities that foreshadow the visit to Mary, another angel asserted the same truth to Abraham and his wife Sarah, in the form of a rhetorical question:

Is anything too hard for the Lord? (Gen. 18:14a, NKJV).

It was a question that Jeremiah the prophet answered, some centuries later when, in an outflow of praise and adoration, he affirmed:

> *'Ah, Lord God! Behold, You have made the heavens and the earth by Your great power and outstretched arm. There is nothing too hard for You.* (Jer. 32:17, NKJV).

We are enlightened repeatedly through Scripture with the vastness of the possibilities that exist for us, through faith in the Bible's God. The great 'I Am Who I Am' (see Exo. 3:14) is unlimited. As noted above, His lovingkindness never stops; His mercies never fail; and He gives His Spirit without limit.

All of these paint a picture of ongoing oversupply. Out of God's unquenchable, tenacious, expansive character, He revealed a Kingdom that embodies the same nature as the King Himself. It will never stop increasing. There is no limit to what He intends to do among humanity and on earth:

> *Of the increase of His government and peace there will be no end.* (Isa. 9:7a, NKJV).

Business implications and application

We've already acknowledged that being a Christian doesn't guarantee immunity from failure or liquidation. Nor does God guarantee that any single business will keep going or expand without limits. Rather it's His Kingdom, where Jesus reigns, that's unlimited. And as we saw in chapter 4, the key 'place' in which the Kingdom of God is evidenced is in human hearts – our hearts.

So, in order to claim the promises of God, we need to be careful that we haven't superimposed our own, corrupted wishes onto His promises. God's declarations of being unlimited don't run to Him being a cosmic genie, on beck and call to do our bidding. Rather, it's we who must align with *His* call, vision, purpose, and Kingdom.

> We need a much bigger appreciation of God, than the picture we currently see.

His lovingkindness, mercies, love, and power are all without limits. As He leads our businesses, we need to believe, know and experience that nothing is impossible with God (see Luke 1:37).

With Jesus as our CEO, our businesses can experience His supply chain in inexhaustible ways. Customers led to us because they need us; deals made available to us; new markets that extend us; staff who inspire us; premises and equipment to grow us; and debt repaid many times over. Our businesses can become so much more than they are at this moment. Dream big!

Likewise, our businesses can offer His supply chain to others in inexhaustible ways. We can invent new ideas, products, manufacturing processes, or even whole new industries. We can grow leaders who take new companies or industries to new heights. We can serve an international community with new realms of compassion and integrity. We can equip and supply countless businesses, livelihoods, ministries and communities. And we can introduce a waiting world to the King Himself, undertaking the works of the Kingdom with courage and without shame:

"Most assuredly, I say to you, he who believes in Me, the works that I do he will do also; and greater works than these he will do, because I go to My Father." (John 14:12, NKJV).

Entrepreneur's Insights (Alistair)

I had already retired at 44, as a multi-millionaire. We'd moved to Canada and back to the UK. My wife decided to ask God to expand our faith. We decided together that we wanted to be in a venture so big that it would fail if God wasn't involved.

In 1998, we had a prophecy to go to Australia, to work with four other people. We sold our house and invested a few million dollars into the company. The four other shareholder investors were all previous CEOs and high-level managers. We believed our business was going to be one of the first trillion dollar companies. It had invented a unique solar concept which produced greater outputs than traditional Photovoltaic products on the market. The product was fantastic and the potential huge. The Australian government made available hundreds of millions of Australian dollars to develop solar farms throughout the country.

Although I was already used to handling large sums of money, we had never done anything this big. We were daunted by the size of it, and realised we needed a much larger vision of who God is. It just seemed too big a project for me to take on, looking at it from an earthly perspective. So my wife and I started to fast and pray. We spent time searching the Scriptures too. I've never searched Scripture so much. As I sought God's word, I asked for revelation. And

God expanded my view of Himself:
-He has a perspective that encompasses cities and nations.
-Abraham was given seed for the whole world.
-Adam was told to name every animal on earth.

As we were interacting at government levels, we felt the need to seek out support people who are Kingdom minded. We got prayer warriors around us: two friends of ours. They'd come and pray with us every week, sometimes for hours. They also came into the project and laid their hands on the equipment.

We were still out of our depth, but kept listening to God. We had to learn to dream. When He gives revelation, you have to act on it — on the dreams, the vision, and the Scriptures. Once you attune yourself to God and align your spirit with His Spirit, you have to move big and fast. But one of our prayer warrior friends reminded us that no one can force God's hand to kick doors in for us — He'll do things in His timing, not ours. So we developed a position we stuck to from then on (and still do): "Peace is the umpire". When there's no peace, we don't move; not until we get His go-ahead.

The company actually failed, and we lost everything. The Australian shareholders proved to be lacking in integrity. When we first arrived, we'd asked to see the financial statements but they didn't want to show them to us. They'd spent all of our seed-money ... and they later lost everything else in the company as well, through gross mis-management of the company's finances. But God had been teaching my wife and me and, when we subsequently returned to the UK, the miracles started happening.

We came back to the UK with only £30,000. We developed a new business idea and proposal, and went to the bank asking for a loan of £1.2m. Whilst the manager was almost laughing at us, his computer suddenly went "ping". An email had just come in saying there was a new European grant for new enterprises – 68% discount on all repayments. He said, "On the basis of this, I can give you your £1.2 m. And the repayments are only going to cost you £600 per month for two years." The timing was miraculous.

Our businesses have increased from there. We now own three companies and are developing the fourth. We have recouped everything we lost in Australia with more besides.

If you're anointed for business, God will put things on to you. You need to stop thinking small, and see Him as an unlimited God, with unlimited resources. His anointing will open doors, governments, finances, and words of influence. You can speak into nations and societies – you can change communities. But you have to be willing to go where it's deeply uncomfortable. That's what a life of faith and surrender does – it calls you out onto the waters, to walk where others won't.

Al Whitmoor-Pryer
Serial entrepreneur, International Trainer
& Business Developer, and Author
Asher Care Ltd & Kahanah Care Ltd
http://www.kahanahcare.co.uk
(United Kingdom)

Demetri's Story

It started with realising how abundant love is. You think you love someone until God takes you to places you didn't even know love could go; when He showers down on you an expression of love that you can't even articulate.

I started my business in my early 30's, when everything seemed good – we were happily married with young children. Some years later, my wife became critically sick. It took more than two years to diagnose because it was so rare. She had a condition that causes inflammation of the cartilage and other tissues – and in her case it meant that she had episodes when she couldn't breathe and would collapse unconscious.

These episodes often meant two weeks in the hospital ICU, and went on from 2005 to approximately 2018. I often had to run my business for weeks from a chair and laptop beside her hospital bed. We had to have some very honest and hard conversation together: we never knew if we'd be going home together, each time she was hospitalized. On discharge days, I felt so blessed. I'd be walking around the hospital full of joy! We'd tell each other: "We made it again this time!"

In 2010, I remember wheeling my wife to a doctor's office in the hospital. She couldn't walk or talk, and I was so tired, caring for her and working at the same time. A nurse commented to me, "We don't usually see this level of love from a husband. Often, when husbands realize they're going to have to go through a long disease with their wife, they can't handle it."

God is infinite. He's unlimited. It's through my wife's illness where I really learned to walk by faith and not by sight; and my business changed beyond recognition.

Law school served me well by giving me a good legal education. Business coaches and marketing advisors did their jobs by teaching me about legal business development. However, experiencing and watching my wife's doctors go beyond the call of duty to help my wife during life-threatening moments added more to my learning. God's way is when you care enough about the person you are serving that you realize it's not about you – it's all about them and what you do to help them in a time of need. It's meeting them where they are, in love, and helping them to see solutions.

One of the changes happened as I watched the way one of my wife's doctors cared for her, treating her in ways that money can't buy. Once I called the doctor's assistant, interrupting a medical school class that he was about to teach. After receiving word from his assistant that I'd called, he cancelled his lecture, and came to the hospital to meet me in person as my wife was being checked into a hospital room. I asked, "Why did you come?" He replied, simply, "Because you called."

I decided I wanted to be a lawyer like he was a doctor! God spoke to my heart: "I've done things for you that are beyond anything you deserve, so you'd better live in a way that starts to do the same for others, alongside Me!"

More than a decade later, I can't tell you how blessed I am. My wife hasn't been in hospital since 2018. Both of our children (a daughter and son) are now adults and are living their best lives. My wife is a successful high school Math instructor and is doing better health-wise than she has done in 15 years; and I am booked solid with legal work for clients. My cup overflows. There is just no limit to what God can and will do.

He lives out His abundance through me, to my clients. Often when people come to me, they think they're after a "smart" lawyer, who'll trap and defeat their opponent. I tell them that I serve Almighty God; that I'll roll my sleeves up and do whatever I need to do, whatever He tells me to do, that's the best for them. And that almost always means resolutions, not combat.

Human conflict strips away God's ability for His glory to shine. When everyone around the table is working to get the "right" outcome, then He reveals the best way forward and the right thing is done. When that happens, everyone experiences God's unlimited love in one way or another; and He gets the glory, as He should!

Demetri Chambers
Walker & Chambers Attorneys at Law
https://www.walkerchambers.com
(United States)

Time-out, for Reflection:

- How has this challenged you to see God's involvement in your business in a new way?
- How can you express His unlimited nature to others, better than you are at present?

CHAPTER 17
THE MIRACULOUS BUSINESS

Nevertheless, lest we offend them, go to the sea, cast in a hook, and take the fish that comes up first. And when you have opened its mouth, you will find a piece of money; take that and give it to them for Me and you."
(Matt. 17:27, NKJV).

What a fun way Jesus offered to Peter, to pay their tax! How practical He is. In everyday business dealings, He takes a deep interest.

From the time God selected the first patriarch of faith, Abraham, He started displaying His 'impossibles', the conception of Isaac being one (see Gen. 18:1-15, and Gen. 21:1-6). Twice, He rescued Sarah miraculously from compromising circumstances into which Abraham had placed her (Gen. 12:10-20[38] and Gen. 20:1-16[39]).

As He formed the Israelite nation out of a bunch of dispirited slaves, He showed up time after time. Leading them through

---

[38] God sent "great plagues" on Pharaoh and his house because Abraham had let Pharoah take Sarah to be an extra wife.

[39] God sent dreams to Abimelech, king of Gerar when, a second time, Abraham let another man take Sarah as his wife.

the Red Sea, defeating their enemies in the same Red Sea, producing water out of a rock, providing manna to eat, writing on stone tablets, appearing in smoke and fire, causing Moses' face to shine . . . the list goes on.

Some time later, Isaiah the prophet recalls these events, then points the Israelites to newer, better, even more miraculous events yet to come:

> *This is what the Lord says—He who made a way through the sea, a path through the mighty waters, ... "Forget the former things; do not dwell on the past. See, I am doing a new thing! Now it springs up; do you not perceive it? I am making a way in the wilderness and streams in the wasteland.* (Isa. 43:16, 18-19, NIV).

> **Time and again throughout both Biblical and practical history, God has overturned physical laws and circumstances, to do the 'impossible' for His people, at individual, local and national levels.**

It's one way He reveals His unbounded love for humanity.

Jesus was clear that we too must expect, and enact, signs and wonders. In His Kingdom, He assumes that the miraculous is in fact the norm. As businesspeople, we need to get our heads around this and start expecting God's miraculous intervention. Rather than wondering whether He really can or will, we need a new perspective: acting as our CEO, why *wouldn't* He use the supernatural power at His disposal to impact the community in which His businesses operate?

> *"Assuredly, I say to you, if you have faith and do not doubt, you will not only do what was done to the fig tree, but also if you say to this mountain, 'Be removed and be cast into the sea,' it will be done. And whatever things you ask in prayer, believing, you will receive."* (Matt. 21:21b-22, NKJV).

Business implications and application

There are so many Biblical accounts of God's involvement in business before Jesus' ministry, e.g.:

- God oversaw the business practices of His people (see Lev. 19; and Prov. 11:1, 16:11, 20:23).
- Abraham's herds and cash-based trading activities prospered immensely (see Gen. 13:2).
- Isaac's arable farm experienced 100% increase in a single year; then experienced further, unusual, ongoing growth – more than anyone would need for personal use (see Gen. 26:12-13).
- After testing Job to the limit and allowing a decimation of his animal husbandry operation (sheep, camels, oxen and donkeys), Job experienced a miraculous duplication of every one of his farmed livestock lines (see Job 1:3; 42:12).
- God interrupted the business activities of cosmological consultants, leading them to a foreign country. There they gave away some of their copious earnings to His Son (see Matt. 2:1-12).

Jesus' ministry shows Him getting miraculously involved in peoples' businesses too, e.g.:

- He helped save the reputation of an inexperienced wedding planner, who'd misquoted on the wine stocks (see John 2:1-12).
- He radically transformed the business practices of a formerly-greedy, dishonest, taxman (see Luke 19:1-10).
- He provided two miraculous catches for Peter and his crews to take to the fish market (see Luke 5:4; and John 21:6).
- He restored a dead widow's son to life, ensuring that he could once again provide for her – financially and otherwise (see Luke 7:11-17).
- Asking Peter to act in faith, Jesus ensured that he could pay his tax (see Matt. 17:27).

Our God specialises in the 'impossible'! Don't short-change yourself by believing or accepting anything less. Press into your relationship with Him, allowing your faith to grow as you choose to let His words abide in you (see John 15:7). Let Jesus start acting miraculously through your business.

Entrepreneur's Insights (Greg)

I learned about God's miraculous provision in business, well before I started running my own business.

As a young manager, I worked for a company that operated a rapid response service for individuals and businesses in South Africa. Violence was common, so our company required all of our officers to wear bullet-resistor vests. One of our officers, I'll call him JC, had been working for us for a while, but I noticed one evening that he wasn't wearing his bullet-resistor that shift. He said it was too warm to wear. I had a strong sense that he needed to (as well as upholding company policy), and insisted that he did. I required him to put it on before I left him.

One hour later, a call came over our radio system saying: "One of our team has been shot". A guard from the complex had seen what had happened: it had been a heartless attack. When I got to the scene, I found it was JC. If he hadn't put on his bullet-resistor, he wouldn't have survived that night. It was clear evidence to me that God was miraculously involved in saving JC's life, intervening just one hour before!

A few years later, I went into the reserve police. Running into danger became a frequent occurrence, to the point where we got so used to it. I even stopped thinking about what might happen. Then, one time, a guy tried to grab me from behind. Amazingly, he just couldn't get to me; he couldn't touch me. Again, I was convinced God was protecting me.

Are you ready to receive business miracles too?

Greg
Entrepreneur and Company Owner
(South Africa)

Robert's Story

My wife, Jerusha, and I travel a lot with our legal nurse consulting business, and we've seen a lot of the people we work with, healed.

Like one guy who was a 20-year old, working on a landscaping crew. The hydraulic line on a concrete truck failed whilst he was nearby. The boom of the truck swung around and hit him on the back of the head. Those things are unbelievably heavy. It was a very serious accident indeed. We were called in for legal consultancy support.

It soon became clear he was paralysed. The doctors were convinced at first that he'd die. Then, when he didn't, they said there was no way he'd ever move any part of his body again, not even his little finger.

Jerusha and I prayed with him during each of our visits. About six months after the incident, he wiggled a toe. It was an amazing moment! Six weeks later he could lift his leg. Today he walks.

He wasn't a Christian at all – but God still blessed Him as we prayed. We've become really close friends with him. We've made sure he knows exactly who's healed him. It'll be a wonderful day when he chooses to follow Jesus.

One of the biggest miracles we see regularly is in our paperwork, strange as that may sound. As part of legal discovery, we're sometimes sent up to 80,000 pages of records by an attorney and told, "Go through those and find 'something'." (Often the attorneys themselves don't know what they want us to find.)

Jerusha and I sit down, place our hands on the records and pray, asking God to help us uncover whatever it is we need to find. Never once has God failed to lead us to what's in there, which needs to be known. Those discoveries are what bring positive resolutions for our clients. God is a God who reveals hidden mysteries, (Dan. 2:47), for the sake of His Name and His glory. It's a privilege to be a worker in His business!

Robert Malaer
Malaer Legal Nurse Consulting, LLC
http://malaerlegalnurseconsulting.com
(United States)

Time-out, for Reflection:

- Have you experienced God's miraculous intervention in your business? Times when He's turned around what seemed impossible odds, providing breakthroughs and miraculous outcomes?
- If that's not been your experience so far, start asking Him for miracles. Embrace His word, to help develop your faith, e.g.:

You do not have because you do not ask. You ask and do not receive, because you ask amiss, that you may spend it on your pleasures. (Jam. 4:2b-3, NKJV).

"Test Me in this," says the Lord Almighty, "and see if I will not throw open the floodgates of heaven and pour out so much blessing that there will not be room enough to store it." (Mal. 3:10b, NIV).

- If you have, praise Him, and ask Him to undertake even more faith-requiring and faith-building miracles – so that Jesus is glorified through your business.

CHAPTER 18
THE EMBRACING BUSINESS

> *The Angel of the Lord called to Abraham from heaven a second time and said..."through your offspring all nations on earth will be blessed, because you have obeyed Me."*
> (Gen. 22:15,18, NIV).

> *"Therefore know that the Lord your God, He is God, the faithful God who keeps covenant and mercy for a thousand generations with those who love Him and keep His commandments."*
> (Deut. 7:9, NKJV).

From the beginning of God's revelation to us in Genesis, He's made plain His longing for all people to know, love, trust, and be blessed by Him. This is the enduring mission of God; to establish unhindered relationship between Himself and us. He seeks us, woos us, then heals us. He, better than anyone, knows that only in Christ, are we restored. We become fully human once more, as He originally intended:

> *The Lord is not slow about His promise, as some count slowness, but is patient toward you, not wishing for any to perish but for all to come to repentance.* (2 Pet. 3:9, NASB 1995).

God recognises our weaknesses and works with them:

> *"A bruised reed He will not break and a dimly burning wick He will not extinguish; He will faithfully bring forth justice."* (Isa. 42:3, NASB 1995).

He is the One who seeks us out, to fulfil His will:

> *"...for the Son of Man has come to seek and to save that which was lost."* (Luke 19:10, NKJV).

> *"If a man has a hundred sheep, and one of them goes astray, does he not leave the ninety-nine and go to the mountains to seek the one that is straying? And if he should find it, assuredly, I say to you, he rejoices more over that sheep than over the ninety-nine that did not go astray. Even so it is not the will of your Father who is in heaven that one of these little ones should perish."* (Matt. 18:12-14, NKJV).

This eternal plan of God for humanity is fulfilled in Jesus, and in Him alone.

Remember His mission? Embrace the poor – give them news of encouragement and restored hope; break addictions and yokes from all those currently captive to them; for all those who are marginalised or oppressed by society – set them free; and proclaim and action favour, to those who currently know little or none (see Luke 4:18-19).

All are welcome through Jesus, the only way God's established (see Heb. 10:20). At His table there's a surplus, which in turn overflows to embrace others (see Psa. 23).

This is in stark contrast to commercial practice, as we explored in chapter 7.

> Commerce will abandon people when they are no longer useful.
>
> The Kingdom of God perpetually includes people.

Brothers and sisters, think of what you were when you were called. Not many of you were wise by human standards; not many were influential; not many were of noble birth. But God chose the foolish things of the world to shame the wise; God chose the weak things of the world to shame the strong. God chose the lowly things of this world and the despised things—and the things that are not—to nullify the things that are, so that no one may boast before Him. (1 Cor. 1:26-29, NIV).

Business implications and application

The disciples are Jesus' leadership team; the ones He's training to take over His mission when He leaves. They're His budding 'C-suite representatives', if you like!

In Mark 9, Jesus uses small children to exemplify His teaching that they must be very careful not to exclude anyone – especially those whom society overlooks and views as invisible or irrelevant:

> *Then He took a little child and set him in the midst of them. And when He had taken him in His arms, He said to them, "Whoever receives one of these little children in My name receives Me; and whoever receives Me, receives not Me but Him who sent Me."* (Mark 9:36-37, NKJV).

John appears to understand, and owns up to a situation where they had seen others who weren't among the main group of disciples, who were ministering in Jesus' Name – and they'd told them to stop (see vv. 38-41).

Sadly, the other disciples appear not to have noted Jesus' instructions. A short while later, in Mark 10, they exercise a 'power-broking and exclusion' role, using their self-assessed credibility as Jesus' disciples to decide who will get to see Him and who won't. Jesus, "greatly displeased", gives them a sharp rebuke:

> *Then they brought little children to Him, that He might touch them; but the disciples rebuked those who brought them. But when Jesus saw it, He was greatly displeased and said to them, "Let the little children come to Me, and do not forbid them; for of such is the kingdom of God. Assuredly, I say to you, whoever does not receive the kingdom of God as a little child will by no means enter it." And He took them up in His arms, laid His hands on them, and blessed them.* (Mark 10:13-16, NKJV).

Take another example. When, centuries ago, God revealed His coming Kingdom to Nebuchadnezzar in a dream, He didn't reveal another battling, earthly regime, where a pretender supplants an old political power with something very similar. No, God's Kingdom looks to *dismantle* the kingdoms of this world, and replace them altogether with one that's fundamentally different: the Kingdom where Jesus is King.

> *And in the days of these kings the God of heaven will set up a Kingdom which shall never be destroyed; and the Kingdom shall not be left to other people; it shall break in pieces and consume all these kingdoms, and it shall stand forever.* (Dan. 2:44, NKJV).

For us in business, this means businesses where Jesus is the CEO.

Kingdom business leaders must learn the joy of being available at all times to embrace anything or anyone, that society dismisses or abandons. God will embrace whom He will embrace – and we must be ready to receive and value them.

Entrepreneur's Insights (Gina)

> *As a company, we use a broker who won't deal with slave growers in the origin countries for our product.*
>
> *We only sell in packaging that is fully recyclable, compostable or refillable.*
>
> *We're a climate-positive company. We offset all the carbon we use + 20%. So the company is already doing more good than would be happening if it didn't exist.*

But we go further. We partner with the government's Ministry of Social Development to assist people into work. Some are considered disadvantaged – for instance, ethnic minorities, single mums, or they may have disabilities.

It's cost us. One lady has come off a disability benefit – she can only work 10 hours a week. She's so faithful: she prays for the mission of our business all the time.

Another lady, a single mum, can only work 20 hours a week, due to health issues. She often needs an hour or so off work for medical appointments etc., so she gets it. She, also, is incredibly faithful, both to us and our mission.

My marketing admin. lady was offered a job with a lot more money than we can pay her (yet!), but she turned it down because she wants to stay with us, helping to fulfil the dream God has given us. She believes in what we're doing, and acknowledges that who we are, is really unusual in business.

If any of them needs an hour off, we offer flexibility, so it's easily arranged. If they need to bring their kids to work, we make that work. We treat them as valued and appreciated people, before treating them as valued and appreciated employees.

Although our business is still relatively young, not yet three years old, God nevertheless oversees all of our growth. I wasn't an accomplished businesswoman when we started, but God is teaching me, as we embrace the attributes of His Kingdom — which includes embracing others. He takes care of the outcomes!

Gina
Online Retail Business Owner/Director
(New Zealand)

Ethan's Story

A number of years ago, I went to China and began a consultancy business there.

On one occasion, I was engaged by a US/Chinese Joint Venture to see if their previously profitable business could be turned around from its present loss-making condition. The majority investors were American entrepreneurs, one of whom managed the company in China. The minority partner was local. None of the investors had professional business experience.

It was a pretty straightforward matter to return the company to profit simply by applying sound financial analysis and modern HR practice. However, what concerned me more was that the company operated illegally in several areas. This was pretty common for privately-owned, small, Chinese businesses, but not for a Foreign-Invested Enterprise.

The American boss, although regarding himself a Christian, took pride in adopting the "Chinese way" of doing business — bribes, tax evasion, under-the-counter deals, and so on. He talked disparagingly of Western executives who 'tried to operate by the book', claiming they could never succeed that way in China.

He'd previously employed a US Consultant to help him; but this didn't last long because the consultant – also a Christian – found some of his skeletons and said that, unless everything was put on a fully-legitimate footing within a month, he would not work there.

I was asked to take on the engagement and, initially, didn't feel sure about working with a corrupt business. So I prayed. God spoke to me through the Biblical story of Daniel. He'd been required to work in the corrupt, Babylonian system and had found a way to do so, even rebuking Nebuchadnezzar a few times! God doesn't shy away from those who don't walk His way – He seeks them and embraces them. I realised God wants Christians to work in corrupt companies, in order to make things better – to be the 'salt and light'.

At first, I had no idea of how we could straighten this company out, because whenever I mentioned 'legalisation' the owner simply said, "We couldn't afford it." Certainly, it seemed outwardly that to start paying full taxes and employee benefits would reduce profits significantly. However, on deeper digging, I believe God revealed a solution to me.

In order to avoid or minimise the various taxes, the owners had established several small-scale companies instead of one large company. Each individual company was below the tax threshold. However, legally, once several companies with the same ownership reach a certain size, under Chinese law they should be amalgamated and pay taxes accordingly. This hadn't happened.

I discovered that, to transfer all the revenue from company to company, and all the various profits into the owners' bank accounts 'under the radar', they were actually paying more in bribes and 'palm-greasing' fees than they would if they started doing everything above-board.

The owner, amazed, would not believe it at first; but finally agreed I was right and decided, "OK, let's go straight from here on". It took nearly two years to bring everything into full compliance with Chinese business and tax laws. During that time God honoured the owner's decision: the profits continued to increase.

For me personally, this engagement led to an important advance in my consulting business, enabling me to develop the speciality of helping local Chinese companies 'go legal'. It's generally believed to be impossible for Chinese nationals to start a business without greasing the palms of various officials. The downside, of course, is that as the companies become successful, these officials have a hold over the owners. Often they end up having to give the officials shares in the company.

I started by getting the owners to set up a brand-new company, and to make sure it remained squeaky clean from Day 1. They could then serve new customers through that entity, whilst continuing to *serve old customers (who were also often corrupt) through the original one.*

As time passed, the business owner could transfer reliable employees to the new company, or recruit fresh ones. As the old company began to underperform, the officials would often want to exit from their involvement or, in some cases, offer to buy it for a song so as to run it themselves. This could rise up to bite them, because under Chinese law, a new owner becomes responsible for all historic misdemeanours dating back seven years. This meant they themselves would become liable if they ever blew the whistle. The original owner was now free from the officials' leverage, and could operate their new, clean companies without hindrance.

I built my consultancy by embracing the 'unlovely' and 'unlovable'; the compromised and corrupt. I embraced them because Jesus embraced them. His embrace got them free. Further, I was able to teach them how to be honest, building characteristics of the Kingdom of God into their new business.

Ethan
Business Consultant in China

Time-out, for Reflection:

- What do you think of Ethan's decision to work with a corrupt person who claims to be a Christian? Where do the challenges lie for you?
- It's not easy to love the unlovely. Jesus did. Think of Him:
    - eating with tax collectors and sinners (see Mark 2:16-17)
    - touching lepers (see Matt. 8:3)

- allowing a prostitute to touch and 'pollute' Him (see Luke 7:36-50).

  How does this affect you? Are you resistant, or willing?
- What softening of your heart is God after, so your business can embrace people whom society ignores?

CHAPTER 19
SO HE ALONE RECEIVES THE GLORY

Jesus... said, "Father, the hour has come; glorify Your Son, that Your Son also may glorify You."

(John 17:1, NKJV).

Now to Him who is able to do exceedingly abundantly above all that we ask or think, according to the power that works in us, to Him be glory in the church by Christ Jesus to all generations, forever and ever. Amen.

(Eph. 3:20-21, NKJV).

It's true that God has enabled the way for us to experience 100% reconciliation, both between us and Himself, and between each other. The blessings and life that flow so easily between the persons of the Trinity reach out to us too, and we're caught up in the blessings of God. Put another way, we share in the overflow of what He's experiencing all the time, as God with God.

But is this the fundamental reason Jesus came? Is that primarily why He died on the Cross – so *we* could be blessed? It's a popular suggestion in our self-focused Western culture . . . but emphatically, no! All the benefits we receive are merely the overspill from the 'main event'.

Jesus came to give glory to His Father. Father and Holy Spirit, recognising His obedience, give glory to Jesus (see Phil. 2:8-11; John 16:13-14; and John 17:1,5).

If nothing else has stuck with you as you've journeyed with me, please, never lose sight of this fact: that Jesus alone needs to be our focus. He is the centre. Not us.

- In Him, all things were created (see Col. 1:16);
- In Him, all things are *gathered* together, both in heaven and on earth (see Eph. 1:10);
- In Him, all things *hold* together (see Col. 1:17);
- In Him, all the fullness of God dwells (see Col. 1:19; and Col. 2:9); and
- In Him, all God's promises are affirmed and confirmed (see 2 Cor. 1:20).

Keep your eyes fixed on Him. We're on deceptive ground when we seek God for what we can get from Him. Our joy comes not from the gifts He gives, but from our relationship with Him, the Giver. His invitation is that we seek *Him*, love *Him*, worship *Him*, find *Him* – because He's worthy.

Even so God, in His mercy, chooses that we will also receive, so that He may have the joy of *sharing* His unbounded love, life, and joy with those He created.

> **"Enter into the joy of your Lord," [Jesus said].**
> **(Matt. 25:23b, NKJV).**

Yes, there is a spill-over; and He offers a remarkable, inclusive promise to us:

> *"I know the plans that I have for you," declares the Lord, "plans for prosperity and not for disaster, to give you a future and a hope. Then you will call upon Me and come and pray to Me, and I will listen to you. And you will seek Me and find Me when you search for Me with all your heart."* (Jer. 29:11-13, NASB).

Why? – For the sole reason that He may receive the glory.

Time-out, for Reflection:

- This could be an ideal opportunity to spend some extended time giving your own thanks, praise, and worship to God – Father, Son and Holy Spirit. He *is* worthy!

CHAPTER 20
THE NEXT MOVE IS YOURS

According to the grace of God which was given to me, as a wise master builder I have laid the foundation....But let each one take heed how he builds on it. For no other foundation can anyone lay than that which is laid, which is Jesus Christ.

Now if anyone builds on this foundation with gold, silver, precious stones, wood, hay, straw, each one's work will become clear...
(1 Cor. 3:10-13a, NKJV).

We began with a question — "What if you make God your CEO, and you become nothing more than His employee?"

What's your choice?

I recently heard someone say: 'The world has changed the Word of God to fit the way we live. We need to change the way we live to fit the Word of God.' I think that's a profound dare to the Western church — and particularly the Christian business community, where we so often applaud God on Sundays and live by other priorities during the business week.

His rightful place in the Kingdom is as its King; His rightful place in your business is as its CEO. The only solid foundation for your business is Jesus Christ.

> *"Therefore whoever hears these sayings of Mine, and does them, I will liken him to a wise man who built his house on the rock…"* (Matt. 7:24, NKJV).

The choice is yours.

If by any chance you don't yet know Jesus, yet you've reached this page, then you can, now. The Kingdom will cost you nothing but will demand everything. The starting point is to ask Him, seek Him and keep knocking until He answers (see Matt. 7:7). Once convicted of your sin, you will – and must – repent (see Acts 2:38). Surrender to Him, in full acceptance of His right to be your King: that's the way we enter His Kingdom. From thereon, it's a wonderful journey of incredible proportions. Hold onto your seat because you're about to be born into an incredible Kingdom! (see John 3:3).

But the foundation of business is only the starting place. On this, your building must be built. Cracks in a foundation undermine the building; whereas a strong foundation allows the whole building to be built strong.

The construction of the building is secondary to laying the foundation. Putting together a successful business, Christian or otherwise, requires multiple learned skills – it's not just about knowing the product or service that you offer. Fortunately, God is a consummate teacher, and teaches us through the written Word, our own experience, the experience of others, speaking direct to our spirits[40], and sometimes through prophetic revelation or words of knowledge and wisdom given us by trusted others.

Be ready to learn – there's a great new journey ahead of you. I'm excited for you, and I have every confidence that God will show you the way, especially once you have surrendered to Him.

I carefully chose a group of trusted mentors, to help me build my business. Without them I wouldn't be where I am today, able to share what I've learned. I've found that having mentors, advisors, and a Godly support team moves me much further, faster. They give an external perspective none of us can gain for ourselves.

Helping businesses grow, improve, and become more profitable is a gift God has given me – I've been doing so successfully for years. If I can help in any way with your business it would be a pleasure and a privilege. (I'm also available as a speaker to business groups, conferences, churches, mission meetings and organisations, and author groups, world-wide). Email me at peter@business-as-mission.com.

You may already have mentors in your current circle of contacts, or you may need professional strategists and coaches, like myself. No modern, professional sports team or person *doesn't* have them – they recognise the powerful value of such support. Even Moses needed input from a

---

[40] See the first book listed in *Further Reading* for a very practical guide on how to hear God's voice.

cultural outsider, Jethro, to compensate for his blind spots, which were leading him to burnout (see Exo. 18:13-22). The problem with blind spots is that, by definition, we don't see them! And whatever we don't – or can't – recognise, we can't change.

Following, you'll find a short list of suggestions for *Further Reading* to start you off, until you choose someone you can trust and connect with at a heart level, who can walk with you side by side.

I'd love you to let me know how your business – and life! – changes over the next weeks, as a result of you developing a deeper relationship with Jesus than ever before. Testimonies of God at work in the lives of others are a great encouragement to the Body of Christ. There's a contact form on my website: https://business-as-mission.com.

Finally – Build true. Build solid. Build with Jesus (not for Him!). Go and be great, in Him:

> ***...the people who know their God shall be strong, and carry out great exploits.* (Dan. 11:32, NKJV).**

ENJOY THIS BOOK?
YOU CAN MAKE A BIG DIFFERENCE.

You, my readers, can have the most incredible and effective impact at getting this book – and the message it contains – widely into the marketplace.

If you believe that others need to hear afresh the significance of God's Kingdom in their lives and businesses (and you've probably already thought of a few people, while you were reading?) then please may I ask you to do three things to help?

Whilst it's still fresh in your mind (perhaps within the next 48 hours), would you consider:-

1) Referring it directly to at least three of your contacts/friends;
2) Emailing me personally at peter@business-as-mission.com, letting me know your thoughts;
3) Writing a review on Amazon (you can search by the book reference number B09MPV8SQP, or by title, or my name).

Thank you so much. I can't tell you how this means to me.

FURTHER READING

Hearing God's Voice

4 Keys to Hearing God's Voice, Copyright © 2010 Mark & Patti Virkler, Pub. Destiny Image Publishers, Inc., P O Box 310, Shippensburg, Pennsylvania 17257-0310, USA.

Hearing God Through Your Dreams: Understanding the Language God Speaks at Night, Copyright © 2016 Dr Mark Virkler and Charity Virkler Kayembe, Pub. Destiny Image Publishers, Inc., P O Box 310, Shippensburg, Pennsylvania 17257-0310, USA.

Faith-Increasing Biographies

Rees Howells: Intercessor, Copyright © 1952 Norman Grubb, Pub. CLC Publications, CLC International (UK), Unit 5, Glendale Avenue, Sandycroft, Flintshire, CH5 2QP, UK.

Daughter of Destiny: Kathryn Kuhlman, Copyright © 1999 Jamie Buckingham, Pub. CBM Australia, 2014, Box Hill, Victoria, Australia.

The Heavenly Man, Copyright © 2002 Chinese Christian Brother Yun with Paul Hattaway, Pub. Monarch Books, Oxford, UK, and Grand Rapids, Michigan, USA.

Holy Spirit Revivals, Copyright © 1964, 1999, 2016 Charles Finney, Pub. Whitaker House, 1030 Hunt Valley Circle, New Kensington, Pennsylvania 15068, USA.

Emotional Maturity in Christ

Emotionally Healthy Spirituality, Copyright © 2008, 2014 Peter L. Scazzero & Geri Scazzero, Pub. Zondervan, 3900 Sparks Drive SE, Grand Rapids, Michigan 49546, USA.

God's Intention to Bless His People Astoundingly

The Prayer of Jabez, Copyright © 2000 Bruce H Wilkinson, Pub. Multnomah Publishers Inc., PO Box 1720, Sisters, Oregon 97759, USA.

The Awesome Power of Blessing, Copyright © 2019, Richard Brunton; and *The Blessing Effect,* Copyright © 2020, Richard Brunton. Both self-published (https://www.richardbruntonministries.org/index.html)

Business As Mission Historical Biographies

Profit for the Lord, Copyright © 1971 William J Danker, Pub. Wipf and Stock Publishers, 150 West Broadway, Eugene, Oregon 97401, USA.

Chocolate Wars, Copyright © 2011 Deborah Cadbury, Pub. Harper Press 77-85 Fulham Palace Road, Hammersmith, London, UK.

Daily Devotional

Experiencing God Day by Day, Copyright © 1998, 2006 Henry T. Blackaby and Richard Blackaby, Pub. B&H Publishing Group, Nashville, Tennessee, USA.

Restoration Year: A 365-Day Devotional, Copyright © 2018 John Eldridge, Pub. Thomas Nelson, HarperCollins Christian Publishing Inc., USA.

ACKNOWLEDGEMENTS

I can't imagine my life without You, my Father. Raised by faithful parents, they introduced me to Your Son at eight. Thank you for baptising me in the Holy Spirit when just 16, and for unfolding my life's adventures ever since. Your presence, grace, guidance, and boundless love are awe-inspiring.

To my wife, Tini, thank you for believing in me. Walking side by side together, your implicit trust in God and in His call to us as a couple is an inspiration to me. Your ability to take my written words and improve my message has also been an inspired gift. I love and cherish you more than words can say.

To every person – family, friend and even adversary – whether you've known it or not, who has led me to understand more about the love and faithfulness of God, thank you. Each of you has driven me resolutely into the arms of my Lord, whose identity I am grateful and proud to embrace.

There are far too many, to name every individual who's added to my life over the years, so I'm forced to limit myself to honouring my four current mentors. Each of you has added incredible value to my life. Graham Moss, my octogenarian friend and prayer warrior: thank you for always speaking the truth to me, insisting that I love Jesus before anyone else. Rob McArthur, you introduced me to a revelation of 'Business as Mission': it's revolutionised my life and business. Johno Melville, your friendship, pastoral insight, excellent coffee and 'deep-bore mining' of Scripture have transformed forever my understanding of Jesus' life and ministry. And Al Whitmoor-Pryer, your entrepreneurial experience and insights persist in bringing blessing after blessing into my life. Thank you all.

To the 35 people who shared your personal stories and business adventures with me, I am indebted. Your experiences have brought this book to life. Sadly, space has not allowed me to include every person's contributions; but every interview was a privilege and it's not been without a lot of difficulty that I've selected the stories which I have. I hope we stay in touch.

To my friends, Chris Martin, Jonathan Cowey, Tim Davis, and again Johno Melville and my longsuffering wife Tini – thank you all for reading portions, or the whole, of my manuscript and for your invaluable improvements. You have enriched the final result beyond measure.

To Debbie Watson, my professional editor, I owe an immense debt of gratitude. You, too, improved my manuscript considerably, and gave your best to my work. Thank you.

I stand in awe of István Szabó, Jene Lubbe and Steve Lloyd (book formatter, cover designer, and photographer respectively) for your extraordinary creativity and commitment.

To my good friend Jan de Lange, for writing the Foreword. Your entrepreneurial skills as owner of international

Acknowledgments

businesses make your words doubly precious to me. Thank you too.

Finally, to you, my readers. If you weren't reading this book, it would be just one more 'white noise' in a world that's already far too full of it. I hope and trust that I am able to add value to you.

ABOUT THE AUTHOR

I've had more than 25 years' SME business experience. Accountancy, the travel sector, family trusts, property development, renovation and trading, import, export, the food industry, transport, mental health, taxis, and business advice and strategy – all have been industries I've embraced and enjoyed. I've been told I have an acute, analytical business mind, an easy-going nature (usually!), and excellent communication skills too. If others are correct, these are gifts, and I can only be immensely grateful.

Such a privileged breadth of experience, combined with my deep faith in Jesus and a prayerfully prophetic perspective on life, allow me to inspire and motivate Christian business owners to build successful Kingdom-based businesses in a way few others do. I'm convinced that God's strategy is to encourage Christian owners to build God-centred, Kingdom-focused, self-sustaining businesses; profitable and fit for His purpose.

For some reason, certain people seem to think that academic qualifications matter – so here goes. I've been a qualified Chartered Accountant Australia and New Zealand (CAANZ) for more than 25 years, a Fellow of the Chartered Association of Certified Accountants (FCCA) for more than 30, and an Associate Fellow of the New Zealand Institute of

Management Southern (AFNZMS) for the past 7. My peers in the national *The Consulting Group,* kindly recognised me as one of their top two performing SME business improvement specialists in New Zealand, from Mar. 2017 to Mar. 2021.

In January 2021, God called me to shift my consulting focus specifically to support Christian businesses across the English speaking world. My role is to help you add discipleship and Biblical growth strategies to your current skill-base. I help owners transform their businesses into expressions of God's Kingdom, with all the associated blessings of obedience to the King (your 'CEO'). I do this through mentoring, both in person and through my books, and as an engaging speaker to business groups, churches and missions, and at conferences.

Born in Kenya, East Africa, I married my wife Tini (originally from the Netherlands) in 2010. Together, we have five wonderful children and six beautiful grandchildren. We're both keen hikers/trampers, and enjoy overseas travel. I'm an avid peanut butter enthusiast (what *doesn't* it go with?!), a lover of well-written novels, a theatre and movie fan, and a (perhaps very!) amateur 'chef'. We're both active members of the second largest Baptist church in NZ's South Island; I oversee the church's prayer ministry, and am privileged to see physical healing and spiritual deliverance on a regular basis. I spent my childhood and teens in Kenya, Hong Kong, Bangladesh, the USA, and the UK, becoming a 'Kiwi' (NZ) citizen in 1998 – a decision I've never regretted.

My readers are always welcome to contact me, either via email (peter@business-as-mission.com) or my business/publishing website (https://business-as-mission.com).

Manufactured by Amazon.ca
Bolton, ON